DEPENDENCE ANALYSIS FOR SUPERCOMPUTING

THE KLUWER INTERNATIONAL SERIES
IN ENGINEERING AND COMPUTER SCIENCE

PARALLEL PROCESSING AND
FIFTH GENERATION COMPUTING

Consulting Editor

Doug DeGroot

Other books in the series:

PARALLEL EXECUTION OF LOGIC PROGRAMS
John S. Conery ISBN 0–89838–194–0

PARALLEL COMPUTATION AND COMPUTERS FOR
ARTIFICIAL INTELLIGENCE
Janusz S. Kowalik ISBN 0–89838–227–0

MEMORY STORAGE PATTERNS IN PARALLEL PROCESSING
Mary E. Mace ISBN 0–89838–239–4

SUPERCOMPUTER ARCHITECTURE
Paul B. Schneck ISBN 0–89838–234–4

ASSIGNMENT PROBLEMS IN PARALLEL
AND DISTRIBUTED COMPUTING
Shahid H. Bokhari ISBN 0–89838–240–8

MEMORY PERFORMANCE OF PROLOG ARCHITECTURES
Evan Tick ISBN 0–89838–254–8

DATABASE MACHINES AND KNOWLEDGE BASE MACHINES
Masaru Kitsuregawa ISBN 0–89838–257–2

PARALLEL PROGRAMMING AND COMPILERS
Constantine D. Polychronopoulos ISBN 0–89838–288–2

DEPENDENCE ANALYSIS FOR SUPERCOMPUTING

by

Utpal Banerjee
Control Data Corporation
Sunnyvale, California

SPRINGER SCIENCE+BUSINESS MEDIA, LLC

Library of Congress Cataloging-in-Publication Data

Banerjee, Utpal, 1942-
  Dependence analysis for supercomputing / by Utpal Banerjee.
  p. cm. — (The Kluwer international series in engineering and computer science. Parallel
processing and fifth generation computing)
  Bibliography: p.
  Includes index.
  ISBN 978-1-4684-6896-0   ISBN 978-1-4684-6894-6 (eBook)
  DOI 10.1007/978-1-4684-6894-6

  1. Supercomputers. 2. Parallel processing (Electronic computers) I. Title. II. Series.
QA76.5.B264 1988   88-13375
004.1′1—dc19   CIP

To my parents:

Santosh Kumar Banerjee
Santi Rani Banerjee

CONTENTS

PREFACE

This book is on dependence concepts and general methods for dependence testing. Here, dependence means data dependence and the tests are compile-time tests. We felt the time was ripe to create a solid theory of the subject, to provide the research community with a uniform conceptual framework in which things fit together nicely. How successful we have been in meeting these goals, of course, remains to be seen. We do not try to include all the minute details that are known, nor do we deal with clever tricks that all good programmers would want to use. We do try to convince the reader that there is a mathematical basis consisting of theories of bounds of linear functions and linear diophantine equations, that levels and direction vectors are concepts that arise rather naturally, that different dependence tests are really special cases of some general tests, and so on.

Some mathematical maturity is needed for a good understanding of the book: mainly calculus and linear algebra. We have covered diophantine equations rather thoroughly and given a description of some matrix theory ideas that are not very widely known. A reader familiar with linear programming would quickly recognize several concepts.

We have learned a great deal from the works of M. Wolfe, and K. Kennedy and R. Allen. Wolfe's Ph. D. thesis at the University of Illinois and Kennedy & Allen's paper on vectorization of Fortran programs are still very useful sources on this subject.

They have done extensive work in this and related areas; they have introduced new concepts and refined old ones. Refinement of the original gcd test and extension of the original inequality test to direction vectors are two examples.

The author is grateful to Prof. David Kuck for introducing him to the subject. He would like to thank Prof. Dan Gajski for encouragement. Prof. David Padua used an early version of the manuscript to teach a class at the University of Illinois and gave many useful comments. The author wants to thank Erwin Huntley, his previous manager at Control Data, for providing the right conditions; Larry Bumgarner, Jack Neuhaus, and Fred Kunz for reading parts of the manuscript; and Rich Ragan and Jeff Lanam for their tremendous help in the mechanics of manuscript preparation.

Any comments of any kind on this book would be very much welcome.

DEPENDENCE ANALYSIS FOR SUPERCOMPUTING

CHAPTER 1

INTRODUCTION

Supercomputers of any given period are, by definition, the fastest computers available in that period. There is a heavy and steadily increasing demand for supercomputers in a wide range of applications that involve huge amounts of data and require enormous computing power. These application areas include meteorology, defense, nuclear energy, petroleum, aerospace, and general scientific research. The parallel processing era started with the realization that sequential computers were reaching their limit because of restrictions imposed by the laws of physics; all supercomputers today use parallel processing in some form. Parallel processing consists in the exploitation of parallelism at one or more levels (i.e., at job, program, subroutine, loop, statement, or

1

instruction level), and its use is not limited to supercomputers alone.

Parallel processing is usually supported in hardware by providing multiple function units, one or more vector pipelines, or a number of CPU's tied together. Parallel languages to support parallel processing have been proposed in recent years, but none has achieved wide acceptance. There is a tremendous investment in existing software packages written in Fortran (and other sequential languages). Even today, programs for supercomputers are written mostly in Fortran (which has been extended by some vendors to include parallel constructs). It is therefore essential to have compilers that can detect and exploit parallelism in sequential programs. At the least, a supercomputer vendor should provide a Fortran compiler that can automatically detect parallelism in a program and generate parallel code by restructuring it to take advantage of the architecture of his machine.

Parallelism detection and program restructuring by a compiler may take the form of vectorization, concurrentization, or a combination of the two. Vectorization means restructuring with the goal of finding vector constructs. An example of such a construct is

$$A(1:100:1) = B(3:102:1) + C(1:199:2)$$

involving three one-dimensional arrays, which is equivalent to the loop

$$
\begin{aligned}
&\textbf{do } I = 1,\ 100 \\
&\qquad A(I) = B(I + 2) + C(2*I - 1) \\
&\textbf{enddo}
\end{aligned}
$$

consisting of a single statement and 100 independent iterations. Concurrentization for multiple processor systems consists in the identification of loops whose different iterations may run simultaneously on different processors, either independently or in an overlapped fashion. For example, the iterations of the following loop may be run simultaneously on a number of processors, provided suitable synchronization support is available for proper processor communication:

$$\textbf{do } I = 1, 100$$
$$B(I) = A(I) + C(I)$$
$$A(I + 2) = D(I) * E(I)$$
$$\textbf{enddo}$$

If processor P_0 is executing iteration $I = i$ and processor P_2 iteration $I = i + 2$, then P_2 must wait until the value of $A(i + 2)$ has been computed by P_0 and is ready for use by P_2.

A restructuring compiler uses a number of program transformations to achieve its goal. Several useful transformations are known today, and some new ones are in the process of being developed. More will probably come in the future to match the evolution of supercomputer architectures. In order to be valid, any particular transformation of a given program must honor the dependence constraints on the memory references in that program. These constraints arise because of the way program variables are defined and used: to ensure correct results, the order in which the definitions and uses of a variable happen must satisfy certain restrictions. It is true in general that the more precise and complete information a compiler has of dependence constraints of a program, the better equipped it is to transform the program in its quest for parallelism. The aim of dependence analysis is to gather useful knowledge about the underlying dependence structure of a program and present it in a convenient form.

The subject has evolved over the years with contributions by a number of authors. The major references are: [Cohagan 1973], [Lamport 1974], [Towle 1976], [Banerjee 1976], [Banerjee et al. 1979], [Banerjee 1979], [Kuhn 1980], [Wolfe 1982], [Allen et al. 1983], [Allen 1983], [Burke & Cytron 1986], [Wolfe & Banerjee 1987], and [Allen & Kennedy 1987]. In this book, we have tried to create a rigorous theory of dependence analysis, incorporating much of the published research and presenting it in a coherent form.

The dependence constraints mentioned above may be viewed as relations between variable occurrences, statements, loop iterations, blocks of statements, etc. We study dependence as a relation between assignment statements. Control-flow considerations are beyond the scope of this book; we take as our program model a Fortran **do** loop consisting of (possibly) other loops and assignment statements. The variables are scalars or (scalar) elements of arrays, and distinct names are assumed to represent distinct variables. The concepts and techniques developed here can be applied to more general programs and other programming languages. Although not necessary for an understanding of the material in this book, some knowledge of the standard program transformations is needed to appreciate why certain specific items of dependence information are computed. (See [Kuck et al. 1981], [Wolfe 1982], [Padua & Wolfe 1986], and [Allen & Kennedy 1987], [Wolfe and Banerjee 1987]. These sources have further references.)

The basic dependence problem is to decide if two indexed elements of an array would represent the same memory location under certain given conditions. A more general problem arises if we consider regions of memory represented in some way and study the possibility of their intersection. Loop indexes being integer variables, these problems reduce to finding integer solutions to a set of diophantine equations subject to a set of inequality constraints. If complete information about this system of equations and inequalities is unavailable at compile-time, the compiler may not be able to do much. Even assuming that the system is fully defined at compile-time, the problem may still be hopeless if nonlinear functions are involved. Fortunately, the subscripts of array elements and limits of loop indexes are usually linear functions in real programs, and we concentrate on this linear problem.

In principle, the existence of dependence in the linear case can be settled by integer programming. There are several methods of inequality elimination that normally would try to find a *real* solution to the system of equations and inequalities and, therefore, be decisive only when there is no real solution. However, all such methods known at present would probably be prohibitively expensive and inefficient in a compiler, given the simplicity of a typical dependence problem and the frequency at which dependence testing is done in a typical situation. We focus on simple practical methods that exploit the special nature of this problem and have been in use for some time. There are exact algorithms that can accurately predict the presence or absence of dependence for certain commonly occurring situations. Even the approximate tests presented here have proved to be quite adequate for real programs. These algorithms (Chapter 6) have been derived systematically from general algorithms that find bounds of linear functions (Chapter 4) and solutions to linear diophantine equations (Chapter 5). The fundamental concepts and the basic notation are developed in chapters 2 and 3.

We should point out here that in many instances, the "proof" of an algorithm is more like an "explanation" or a "demonstration." The examples form a very important part of the book; if the programs in some of them appear to be artificial, that is because they are designed to be compact, yet representative of specific situations.

The remainder of this chapter consists of a set of examples which should give the reader a glimpse of the material described in the later chapters. Each example presents a program consisting of loops and assignment statements. Remember that each loop is supposed to be executed sequentially, imposing some constraints on the order of memory references in the program, which we are trying to find and analyze.

Example 1.1.

$$\begin{array}{ll}
 & \textbf{do } I = 1, 100 \\
\text{S:} & \quad A(I) = B(I + 2) + 1 \\
\text{T:} & \quad B(I) = A(I - 1) - 1 \\
 & \textbf{enddo}
\end{array}$$

For each value i of I in {1, 2,..., 100}, there is an instance of statement S and an instance of statement T, which we denote by S(i) and T(i), respectively. To see exactly how different elements of the arrays A, B, C are referenced by the instances, it helps to partially unroll the loop, as shown in Table 1.1. The value of the element A(1) computed by the instance S(1) is used by the instance T(2), the value of A(2) computed by S(2) is used by T(3), and so on. In general, the value of A(i) computed by S(i) is used by T(i + i), $1 \le i$

≤ 99. This makes statement T *flow-dependent* on statement S; in symbols, S δ^f T. The variables A(I) of S and A(I − 1) of T *cause* this dependence. The set of iteration pairs *associated* with this dependence is

$$\{(i, j): j = i + 1, \ 1 \le i \le 99\}.$$

There is a constant *dependence distance* of 1, since $j − i = 1$ for each pair.

The value of B(3) used by S(1) is the value that existed before the execution of the loop, and not the one computed by T(3). In other words, S(1) must use the value of B(3) before it is changed by T(3). Similarly, S(2) must use the value of B(4) before it is changed by T(4), and so on. In general, S(i) must use the value of B(i + 2) before it is changed by T(i + 2), $1 \le i \le 98$. That makes T *anti-dependent* on S; in symbols, S δ^a T. This anti-dependence is caused by the variables B(I + 2) of S and B(I) of T. The associated set of iteration pairs is

$$\{(i, j): j = i + 2, \ 1 \le i \le 98\}.$$

We again have a constant dependence distance, namely 2.

Table 1.1. Loop of Example 1.1 after unrolling.

S(1):	A(1)	= B(3) + 1
T(1):	B(1)	= A(0) − 1
S(2):	A(2)	= B(4) + 1
T(2):	B(2)	= A(1) − 1
S(3):	A(3)	= B(5) + 1
T(3):	B(3)	= A(2) − 1
S(4):	A(4)	= B(6) + 1
T(4):	B(4)	= A(3) − 1
		⋮
S(100):	A(100)	= B(102) + 1
T(100):	B(100)	= A(99) − 1

If we first execute all iterations of S simultaneously and next all iterations of T simultaneously, then T uses the correct values of A(1), A(2),..., A(99) computed by S, and S uses the values of B(3), B(4),..., B(102) before they are changed by T.

Example 1.2.

$$\textbf{do } I = 1,\ 100$$

T: $C(I) = A(3*I + 1) + 1$
S: $A(2*I + 7) = B(I) - 3$

$$\textbf{enddo}$$

The variables $A(2I + 7)$ and $A(3I + 1)$ may cause a flow-dependence of statement T on statement S. It is not immediately clear if T is really dependent on S and, if it is, which iterations are involved or what is a dependence distance in this case. Unrolling the loop completely would provide the answers, but there is a better and analytical way. An instance $T(j)$ of T uses the value computed by an instance $S(i)$ of S, iff iteration $I = j$ comes after iteration $I = i$ and the variables $A(2i + 7)$ and $A(3j + 1)$ are identical, i.e., iff $i < j$, and

$$2i + 7 = 3j + 1 \quad \text{or} \quad 2i - 3j = -6.$$

This is a linear diophantine equation in two integer variables. Since i, j are values of the index variable I, they must also satisfy

$$1 \le i \le 100 \quad \text{and} \quad 1 \le j \le 100.$$

If there is an integer solution (i, j) to the equation satisfying all these conditions, then the variables $A(2I + 7)$ of statement S and $A(3I + 1)$ of statement T make T flow-dependent on S. The general solution, in case it exists, will give all the iteration pairs involved in the dependence and also the dependence distances. (There may not always be a constant dependence distance.)

Note that the same pair of variables could make statement S anti-dependent on statement T. The roles of i and j are reversed in this case. If the notation is unchanged, the same equation is to be solved under the same constraints with one exception: instead of $i < j$, we want $j \le i$, since now the variable $A(3j + 1)$ is to be referenced before the variable $A(2i + 7)$.

Example 1.3.

$$\textbf{do } I_1 = 1, 100$$
$$\quad \textbf{do } I_2 = 1, 50$$
$$\text{S:} \qquad A(I_1, I_2) = A(I_1, I_2 - 1) + B(I_1, I_2)$$
$$\quad \textbf{enddo}$$
$$\textbf{enddo}$$

Consider first the ordering of iterations of this double loop. An iteration $(I_1, I_2) = (i_1, i_2)$ precedes an iteration $(I_1, I_2) = (j_1, j_2)$ in one of two ways:

$$i_1 < j_1, \qquad \text{or} \qquad i_1 = j_1 \text{ and } i_2 < j_2.$$

The value computed by S in an iteration (i_1, i_2) is same as the value used in an iteration (j_1, j_2), iff $A(i_1, i_2)$ and $A(j_1, j_2 - 1)$ represent the same variable, i.e., iff $i_1 = j_1$ and $i_2 = j_2 - 1$. Thus, the value computed in an iteration (i_1, i_2) is used in a later iteration (j_1, j_2) where $i_1 = j_1$ and $i_2 < j_2$. This is expressed by saying that S is flow-dependent on itself at *level* 2. We could also say that S is flow-dependent on itself with a *direction vector* $(0, 1)$, since 0 is the sign of $(j_1 - i_1)$ and 1 the sign of $(j_2 - i_2)$ for each associated iteration pair (i_1, i_2), (j_1, j_2). (The numerical definition of sign is given in Section 2.2.)

Example 1.4.

$$\textbf{do } I_1 = 1, 100$$
$$\quad \textbf{do } I_2 = 1, 50$$
$$\text{S:} \qquad A(I_1 + 2, I_2) = A(I_1, I_2 + 3) + B(I_1, I_2)$$
$$\quad \textbf{enddo}$$
$$\textbf{enddo}$$

The value computed by S in an iteration (i_1, i_2) will be used in an iteration (j_1, j_2), iff the variables $A(i_1 + 2, i_2)$ and $A(j_1, j_2 + 3)$ are the same, i.e., iff $i_1 + 2 = j_1$ and $i_2 = j_2 + 3$. Thus, the value computed in an iteration (i_1, i_2) is used in an iteration (j_1, j_2) where $i_1 < j_1$. That means S depends on itself at level 1. Since $i_1 < j_1$ and $i_2 > j_2$, more detailed information is conveyed if we say that S is dependent on itself with direction vector $(1, -1)$. This dependence is caused by the output variable $A(I_1 + 2, I_2)$ and the input variable $A(I_1, I_2 + 3)$. The associated set of iteration pairs is

$$\{((i_1, i_2), (j_1, j_2)): j_1 = i_1 + 2, \ j_2 = i_2 - 3, \ 1 \le i_1 \le 98, \ 4 \le i_2 \le 50\}.$$

There is also a constant distance vector of $(2, -3)$, since $j_1 - i_1 = 2$ and $j_2 - i_2 = -3$ for each iteration pair in the set. The reader should convince himself that there is no dependence at level 2.

Example 1.5.

```
        do I₁ = 1, 100
          do I₂ = 1, 50
S:              A(3*I₁ + 2, 2*I₂ − 1) = A(5*I₂, I₁ + 3) + 1
          enddo
        enddo
```

If the subscripts are complicated, one must use analytical methods for checking dependence. For example, in order to decide if S depends on itself at level 1 with direction vector $(1, -1)$, we need to solve the system of linear diophantine equations

$$3i_1 - 5j_2 = -2$$
$$2i_2 - j_1 = 4$$

where the (integer) variables satisfy the conditions

$$1 \le i_1 \le 100, \quad 1 \le i_2 \le 50,$$
$$1 \le j_1 \le 100, \quad 1 \le j_2 \le 50,$$

$$i_1 < j_1,$$
$$i_2 > j_2.$$

Example 1.6.

$$\textbf{do } I_1 = 1, 100$$
$$\quad \textbf{do } I_2 = 1, 50$$

S:
$$\qquad A(3*I_1 + 2*I_2 - 1) = B(I_1, I_2) - 1$$

T:
$$\qquad A(-I_1 - 5*I_2) = C(I_1, I_1)$$

$$\quad \textbf{enddo}$$
$$\textbf{enddo}$$

There is another kind of dependence that we have not illustrated so far. Statement T is *output-dependent* on statement S, (S δ^o T), if there are iterations (i_1, i_2) and (j_1, j_2) such that $S(i_1, i_2)$ and $T(j_1, j_2)$ both compute values of the same variable and the value computed by $T(j_1, j_2)$ is to be stored after the value computed by $S(i_1, i_2)$. This is true if iteration (i_1, i_2) precedes or is identical to iteration (j_1, j_2), and the variables $A(3i_1 + 2i_2 - 1)$ and $A(-j_1 - 5j_2)$ are the same. As before, we have a linear diophantine equation

$$3i_1 + j_1 + 2i_2 + 5j_2 = 1,$$

with some constraints, namely

$$1 \le i_1 \le 100, \quad 1 \le i_2 \le 50,$$
$$1 \le j_1 \le 100, \quad 1 \le j_2 \le 50;$$

and

either
$$i_1 < j_1,$$

or
$$i_1 = j_1, \quad i_2 \le j_2.$$

Sometimes, it is difficult to decide exactly if an equation or a system of equations has a solution satisfying a given set of constraints. We then resort to approximate methods which test necessary conditions for the existence of such solutions. One such method that has been found to be very efficient in practical applications would work in this case as follows: Find a set of lower and upper bounds of the linear function $(3i_1 + j_1 + 2i_2 + 5j_2)$ in the region defined by the above conditions on the variables. If the right hand side of the equation, (i.e., the integer 1) fails to lie between these bounds, then there is no solution satisfying the conditions, and hence no dependence. Suppose that 1 does fall between the bounds. Even if the bounds are the extreme values of the function in the region, all we can conclude is that there is a *real* solution satisfying the conditions (via the Intermediate Value Theorem of Advanced Calculus, stated as Theorem 4.1.1 in Section 4.1). We assume in this case that an integer solution also exists, to be on the safe side. (An unnecessary dependence may result in a loss of parallelism, but will not lead to false code.)

Example 1.7.

$$
\begin{array}{ll}
S_1: & x = y + 1 \\
& \textbf{do } I = 2, 30 \\
S_2: & \quad C(I) = x + B(I) \\
S_3: & \quad A(I) = C(I - 1) + z \\
S_4: & \quad C(I + 1) = B(I) * A(I) \\
& \quad \textbf{do } J = 2, 50 \\
S_5: & \quad\quad F(I, J) = F(I, J - 1) + x \\
& \quad \textbf{enddo} \\
& \textbf{enddo} \\
S_6: & z = y + 3
\end{array}
$$

Here we have the following dependence relations:

$$
\begin{array}{llll}
S_1 \, \delta^f S_2, & S_1 \, \delta^f S_5, & S_2 \, \delta^f S_3, & S_3 \, \delta^f S_4, \\
S_3 \, \delta^a S_6, & S_4 \, \delta^o S_2, & S_4 \, \delta^f S_3, & S_5 \, \delta^f S_5.
\end{array}
$$

The dependence structure of the program is conveniently described by its *dependence graph*: a directed graph with six nodes representing the six statements, such that there is an arc from a node S_k to a node S_l iff S_l depends on S_k in some way (Figure 1.1). Usually, we denote flow-dependence by a plain arc, anti-dependence by a crossed arc, and output-dependence by an arc with a small circle on it.

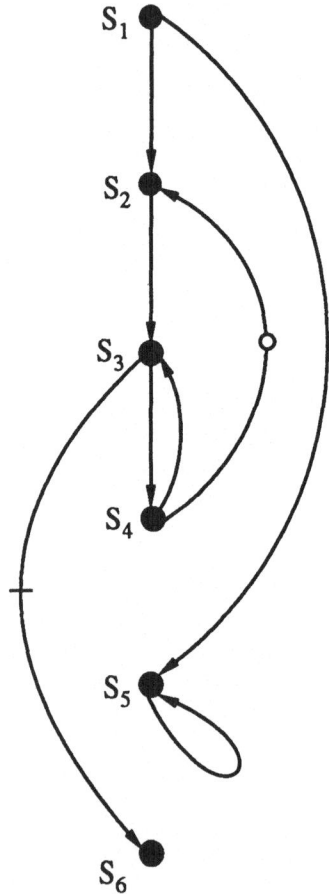

Fig. 1.1. Dependence Graph for Example 1.7.

CHAPTER 2

BASIC CONCEPTS

We assume that the reader is familiar with relations and their graphs. The first section of this chapter gives some of the elementary definitions in this area; for more detail, consult any standard books on set theory and graph theory. We would recommend [Halmos 1965] for relations and [Knuth 1974] for graphs. Order relations on vectors are studied in Section 2.2; they are useful in understanding the ordering of loop iterations which plays a very important role in dependence analysis. We introduce direction vectors in the same section and show how they represent those relations. Finally, Section 2.3 describes the program model we are going to use; the goal here is to establish notation for various loop nests containing assignment statements in the program.

2.1. RELATIONS AND GRAPHS

A *relation* R in a set S is a set of ordered pairs of elements of S. If (a, b) ∈ R, we write a R b. The *inverse* of a relation R, denoted by R^{-1}, is obtained by reversing each of the pairs belonging to R, so that a R^{-1} b iff b R a. Let R denote the union and R´ the inter-section of a nonempty collection of relations $\{R_k: k ∈ C\}$ in S. Then a R b means a R_k b for some k ∈ C, and a R´ b means a R_k b for each k ∈ C. A relation R in S is

reflexive, if a R a for every a in S;
irreflexive, if a R a is false for every a in S;
symmetric, if a R b implies that b R a;
antisymmetric, if a R b and b R a imply that a = b;
transitive, if a R b and b R c imply that a R c.

The transitive closure $\overline{R}$ of a relation R in S is the smallest transi-tive relation in S containing R. We have a $\overline{R}$ b, iff there is a se-quence $a_1, a_2,..., a_n$ of elements of S such that

$$a = a_1, \quad a_1 R a_2, \quad a_2 R a_3,..., \quad a_{n-1} R a_n, \quad a_n = b.$$

A relation is an *equivalence relation* if it is reflexive, symmetric and transitive. Let R denote an equivalence relation in a set S. If a ∈ S, the *equivalence class* of a with respect to R is the set of all those elements b in S for which a R b. These classes form a parti-tion of S, i.e., they are a collection of nonempty, pairwise disjoint subsets whose union is S.

A relation is a *partial order* if it is reflexive, antisymmetric and transitive. A partial order is usually denoted by the symbol ≤. For every partial order ≤ in a set S, there is a corresponding irreflexive and transitive relation < in S, defined as follows: for a, b ∈ S, we have a < b if a ≤ b and a ≠ b. Conversely, from any irreflexive and transitive relation < in S, a partial order ≤ can be constructed by requiring that a ≤ b if either a < b or a = b. We say that < is the *strict* relation corresponding to ≤, and ≤ is the *weak* relation corresponding to <.

A *partially ordered set* is a set together with a partial order in it. Suppose $(S, \leq)$ is a partially ordered set and a, b are elements of S. If a < b, we say that a is a *predecessor* of b and b is a *successor* of a. If a < b and there is no c such that a < c < b, then a is an *immediate predecessor* of b and b is an *immediate successor* of a. The elements a and b are *comparable* if either a = b, or a < b, or b < a. If S has an element a such that $a \leq x$ for all x in S, then a is the *least element* of S. An element a is a *minimal element* if x < a is false for all x in S. One can similarly define the greatest element and a maximal element of S. A subset P of S is a *chain* if any two elements in P are comparable; it is an *antichain* if no two distinct elements in P are comparable. The *length* of a chain is the number of elements in it. A chain (antichain) is *maximal* if it is not a proper subset of any chain (antichain).

A *total order* in a set S is a partial order such that any two elements of S are always comparable, i.e., the entire set S is one chain. A *totally ordered set* is a set with a total order in it.

A *directed graph* consists of a set of nodes and a set of arcs, each arc leading from a node u to a node v. If e is an arc from u to v, we say that the *initial node* of e is u, the *final node* of e is v, and we write u = init(e), v = fin(e). An arc is a *self-loop* if its initial and final nodes are the same. Two arcs are *antiparallel* if the final node of each is the initial node of the other. The *out-degree* out(v) of a node v is the number of arcs leading from it, and the *in-degree* in(v) of v is the number of arcs leading to it. A node v is a *source* if in(v) = 0, a *sink* if out(v) = 0. For $n \geq 1$, a *path* of length n is a sequence of arcs $(e_1, e_2,..., e_n)$ such that $\text{fin}(e_k) = \text{init}(e_{k+1})$, $1 \leq k < n$. Such a path is said to be *from* u *to* v, where u = init(e_1) and v = fin(e_n). A *cycle* is a path $(e_1, e_2,..., e_n)$ such that $\text{fin}(e_n) = \text{init}(e_1)$. A graph is *acyclic* if it has no cycles; it is *cyclic* otherwise.

To each relation R in a set S, there corresponds a directed graph G whose nodes represent the elements of S, and such that there is an arc in G directed from a node a to a node b iff a R b. We say that G is the *graph* of the relation R.

2.2. ORDERS ON VECTORS

Let $\mathbf{R}$ denote the set of real numbers and $\mathbf{Z}$ the set of integers. The *signum* function sig: $\mathbf{R} \to \mathbf{Z}$ is defined by

$$\text{sig}(x) = \begin{cases} -1 & \text{if } x < 0 \\ 0 & \text{if } x = 0 \\ 1 & \text{if } x > 0 \end{cases}$$

for $x \in \mathbf{R}$. Consider $\mathbf{R}^n$, the set of all real n-vectors, where $n \geq 1$. The zero vector $(0, 0,..., 0)$ is denoted by $\mathbf{0}$. For $1 \leq u \leq n$, define a relation $<_u$ in $\mathbf{R}^n$ by requiring that two vectors $\mathbf{i} = (i_1, i_2,..., i_n)$ and $\mathbf{j} = (j_1, j_2,..., j_n)$ satisfy $\mathbf{i} <_u \mathbf{j}$ iff

$$i_1 = j_1, \quad i_2 = j_2,..., \quad i_{u-1} = j_{u-1}, \quad \text{and} \quad i_u < j_u.$$

For example, we have $(1, 3) <_1 (2, -4)$ and $(1, 2) <_2 (1, 3)$ in $\mathbf{R}^2$. Let $<$ denote the union of the relations $<_u$ for $1 \leq u \leq n$; it is called the *lexicographic order* in $\mathbf{R}^n$. Basic properties of $<_u$ and $<$ are given in Lemma 2.2.1.

Lemma 2.2.1. Let $n \geq 1$, and let $\mathbf{i}, \mathbf{j}, \mathbf{k}$ denote arbitrary vectors in $\mathbf{R}^n$.

1. For each u in $1 \leq u \leq n$, the relation $<_u$ in $\mathbf{R}^n$ is irreflexive and transitive, so that the corresponding weak relation $\leq_u$ is a partial order.

2. The n relations $<_u$ are pairwise disjoint: $\mathbf{i} <_u \mathbf{j}$ and $\mathbf{i} <_v \mathbf{j}$ imply that $u = v$.

3. If $\mathbf{i} \neq \mathbf{j}$, there is a unique integer u such that $1 \leq u \leq n$ and exactly one of the following two conditions holds: $\mathbf{i} <_u \mathbf{j}$ or $\mathbf{j} <_u \mathbf{i}$.

4. $\mathbf{i} <_u \mathbf{j}$ and $\mathbf{j} <_v \mathbf{k}$ together imply that $\mathbf{i} <_w \mathbf{k}$, where $w = \min(u, v)$.

5. The relation $<$ in $\mathbf{R}^n$ is irreflexive and transitive, and the corresponding weak relation $\leq$ is a total order in $\mathbf{R}^n$.

PROOF. All five parts follow easily from the definitions. Only parts 1, 3, and 5 are proved here; the other two are left to the reader.

We consider three arbitrary n-vectors:

$$\mathbf{i} = (i_1, i_2,..., i_n), \quad \mathbf{j} = (j_1, j_2,..., j_n), \quad \mathbf{k} = (k_1, k_2,..., k_n).$$

Part 1. One implication of $\mathbf{i} <_u \mathbf{i}$ is that $i_u < i_u$ which is false. Hence, the relation $<_u$ is irreflexive. Again, $\mathbf{i} <_u \mathbf{j}$ and $\mathbf{j} <_u \mathbf{k}$ mean that

$$i_1 = j_1, \quad i_2 = j_2,..., \quad i_{u-1} = j_{u-1}, \quad \text{and} \quad i_u < j_u$$

and

$$j_1 = k_1, \quad j_2 = k_2,..., \quad j_{u-1} = k_{u-1}, \quad \text{and} \quad j_u < k_u,$$

which imply

$$i_1 = k_1, \quad i_2 = k_2,..., \quad i_{u-1} = k_{u-1}, \quad \text{and} \quad i_u < k_u,$$

i.e., $\mathbf{i} <_u \mathbf{k}$. This proves that the relation $<_u$ is transitive.

Part 3. Let $\mathbf{i} \neq \mathbf{j}$. Then we cannot have $i_r = j_r$ for each r in $1 \leq r \leq n$. Let u denote the smallest positive integer such that $i_u \neq j_u$. Then

$$i_1 = j_1, \quad i_2 = j_2,..., \quad i_{u-1} = j_{u-1}.$$

If $i_u < j_u$, we have $\mathbf{i} <_u \mathbf{j}$; otherwise $\mathbf{j} <_u \mathbf{i}$.

Part 5. The relation $<$ is irreflexive, since $\mathbf{i} < \mathbf{i}$ means $\mathbf{i} <_u \mathbf{i}$ for some u, which is ruled out by (1). If we have $\mathbf{i} < \mathbf{j}$ and $\mathbf{j} < \mathbf{k}$, then by definition, $\mathbf{i} <_u \mathbf{j}$ and $\mathbf{j} <_v \mathbf{k}$ must hold for some u, v. It then follows from part 4 that $\mathbf{i} <_w \mathbf{k}$ where $w = \min(u, v)$, i.e., $\mathbf{i} < \mathbf{k}$. Thus, the relation $<$ is transitive. The corresponding weak relation $\leq$ is then a partial order. In fact, part 3 implies that $\leq$ is a total order, since for any two distinct vectors $\mathbf{i}, \mathbf{j}$, we must have either $\mathbf{i} < \mathbf{j}$ or $\mathbf{j} < \mathbf{i}$. ♦

If we extend the definition of $<_u$ naturally to the case $u = n + 1$, then $\mathbf{i} <_{n+1} \mathbf{j}$ would mean $i_r = j_r$ for each r in $1 \leq r \leq n$, i.e., $\mathbf{i} = \mathbf{j}$. As we shall see later on, it is sometimes notationally convenient to use $<_{n+1}$ to denote equality among vectors. Although the same symbols $<$ and $\leq$ are used for order relations in both scalars and vectors, no confusion should result, since the context and/or the notation would always make the nature of the arguments clear.

We will use $>$ to denote the inverse of the relation $<$ in $\mathbf{R}^n$. The first nonzero element of a vector is called its *leading element*. A vector $\mathbf{i}$ is *negative* if $\mathbf{i} < \mathbf{0}$, i.e., if it has a negative leading element. Similarly, $\mathbf{i}$ is *positive* if $\mathbf{i} > \mathbf{0}$, which means $\mathbf{i}$ has a positive leading element. For an ordered pair of vectors $(\mathbf{i}, \mathbf{j})$, where $\mathbf{i} = (i_1, i_2, ..., i_n)$ and $\mathbf{j} = (j_1, j_2, ..., j_n)$, the *distance vector* is

$$(j_1 - i_1, j_2 - i_2, ..., j_n - i_n),$$

and the *direction vector* is

$$\mathbf{s} = \big(\text{sig } (j_1 - i_1), \text{sig}(j_2 - i_2), ..., \text{sig}(j_n - i_n)\big).$$

Thus, the rth element of $\mathbf{s}$ is 1, 0, or -1 according as i_r is less than, equal to, or greater than j_r. It is often convenient to deal with *incompletely specified direction vectors* that represent sets of direction vectors. For example, the set

$$\big\{(0, 0, 0, 1), (0, -1, 0, 1), (0, 0, 1, 1), (0, -1, 1, 1)\big\}$$

may be represented by the (incompletely specified) direction vector $(0, \leq0, \geq0, 1)$. Similarly, denoting "don't care" by $*$, we may represent the set

$$\big\{(0, -1, 0, -1), (0, 0, 0, -1), (0, 1, 0, -1)\big\}$$

by $(0, *, 0, -1)$. Given the distance vector we can compute the direction vector (but not the other way around): the direction vector is obtained from a distance vector $(\lambda_1, \lambda_2, ..., \lambda_n)$ by taking the signs of $\lambda_1, \lambda_2, ..., \lambda_n$. Thus, if the distance vector of a pair of vectors in $\mathbf{R}^3$ is $(2, -3, 0)$, the corresponding direction vector will be $(1, -1, 0)$. The usefulness of direction vectors comes from the fact that they describe the order relation between two vectors in a convenient way:

Lemma 2.2.2. Let i, j denote two vectors in $\mathbf{R}^n$ and s their direction vector. Then $i < j$ iff $s > 0$, iff s has one of the following n forms:

$$(1, *, *,..., *)$$
$$(0, 1, *,..., *)$$
$$(0, 0, 1, *,..., *)$$
$$\vdots$$
$$(0, 0,..., 0, 1).$$

More precisely, $i <_u j$ for a u in $1 \leq u \leq n$, iff s has the form with a leading 1 after $(u - 1)$ zeros.

PROOF. Since $i < j$ holds iff $i <_u j$ for some u in $1 \leq u \leq n$, it is sufficient to prove the second part.

For $i = (i_1, i_2,..., i_n)$ and $j = (j_1, j_2,..., j_n)$, we have $i <_u j$
iff
$$i_1 = j_1, \quad i_2 = j_2,..., \quad i_{u-1} = j_{u-1}, \quad \text{and} \quad i_u < j_u;$$
iff
$$sig(j_1 - i_1) = sig(j_2 - i_2) = \cdots = sig(j_{u-1} - i_{u-1}) = 0$$
and
$$sig(j_u - i_u) > 0;$$

i.e., iff s has a leading 1 after $(u - 1)$ zeros. ◆

Example 2.2.1. Consider vectors in $\mathbf{R}^4$. We have

$$(1, 2, 3, 4) \ <_1 \ (2, 0, 0, 0)$$
$$(1, 2, 3, 4) \ <_2 \ (1, 3, -1, 0)$$
$$(1, 2, 2, 3) \ <_3 \ (1, 2, 3, 3)$$
$$(1, 2, 2, 3) \ <_4 \ (1, 2, 2, 13)$$
$$(1, 2, 2, 4) \ <_5 \ (1, 2, 2, 4).$$

For the pair $\big((1, 2, 3, 4,), (1, 3, -1, 0)\big)$, the distance and direction vectors are $(0, 1, -4, -4)$ and $(0, 1, -1, -1)$, respectively. Note that $(0, 1, -1, -1)$ fits the form $(0, 1, *, *)$.

The standard notation for direction vectors seen in the literature uses $<, =, >$ for $1, 0, -1$, respectively, so that, for example, the direction vector $(0, 1, -1)$ would be written as $(=, <, >)$. This notation is convenient for writing incompletely specified direction vectors; for example, $(\leq, >)$ represents the set $\{(<, >), (=, >)\}$. However, it sometimes leads to clumsiness, as in the sentence: "The direction vector is (s_1, s_2, s_3) where $s_1 = <$, $s_2 = =$, and $s_3 = \geq$." The reader should feel free to use the notation he is comfortable with.

2.3. PROGRAM MODEL

Our program model allows only **do** loops and assignment statements. This framework is quite adequate for the development of our theory. It lets us concentrate on the problem of comparing memory references generated by indexed array elements without having to worry about control flow and other considerations required by a more general program. The concepts and results, however, can be extended to the general situation.

A *variable* is either a scalar or a (scalar) element of an array. An *assignment statement* S has the form

$$\text{S:} \qquad x = E$$

where x is a variable and E an expression. The *output variable* of S is x and its *input variables* are the variables in E. The set containing the output variable is denoted by OUT(S) and the set of input variables by IN(S).

A *loop* is a **do** loop of the form

$$L: \qquad \textbf{do } I = p, q$$
$$H$$
$$\textbf{enddo}$$

where p, q are integer-valued expressions and H is a sequence of
loops and assignment statements. For this loop, the *index* is I, the
lower limit is p, the *upper limit* is q, and the *body* is H. There are
$(q - p + 1)$ iterations of the loop corresponding to the values $I = p$,
$p + 1,...,$ q, and they are to be executed in that order in the serial
execution of L.

A *nest* L of *length* m is a sequence of m loops $(L_1, L_2,..., L_m)$
such that L_k contains L_{k+1}, and there is no third loop contained in
L_k that also contains L_{k+1}, $(1 \leq k \leq m - 1)$. The *index*, the *lower
limit*, and the *upper limit* of L are three m-vectors I, p, and q, respectively, defined by

$$\mathbf{I} = (I_1, I_2,..., I_m)$$
$$\mathbf{p} = (p_1, p_2,..., p_m)$$
$$\mathbf{q} = (q_1, q_2,..., q_m)$$

where I_k is the index variable and p_k, q_k the lower and upper limits
of the kth loop L_k, $(1 \leq k \leq m)$. The *iteration space* of nest L is the
following subset of $\mathbf{Z}^m$, the set of integer m-vectors:

$$\left\{ (I_1, I_2,..., I_m) \in \mathbf{Z}^m : p_1 \leq I_1 \leq q_1, \ p_2 \leq I_2 \leq q_2,..., \ p_m \leq I_m \leq q_m \right\}.$$

Each point in this space represents an iteration of the loop nest. If
the loop limits are invariant within the nest, the number of points is
$\prod_{k=1}^{m}(q_k - p_k + 1)$. In the serial execution of the nest, an itera-
tion $\mathbf{I} = \mathbf{i}$ precedes an iteration $\mathbf{I} = \mathbf{j}$ iff $\mathbf{i} < \mathbf{j}$. The nest is *perfect* if
the body of L_k is just L_{k+1}, $(1 \leq k \leq m - 1)$. For a perfect nest, the
body of the innermost loop L_m is often referred to as the body of
the nest.

Consider a program which is a sequence of loops and assignment statements; each loop may contain assignment statements
and/or more loops. Without any loss in generality, we assume that
the whole program is itself a loop, probably a trivial loop with a

single iteration. Let S denote an arbitrary assignment statement in the program. The set of all loops containing S, ordered from the outermost to the innermost loop, is a nest; call it **nest(S)**. If **I** denotes the index of this nest, we sometimes write S(**I**) for S to emphasize the fact that the index variables of **nest(S)** generally appear in S. For a given iteration **I** = **i** of **nest(S)** we get a particular instance of S(**I**), which is denoted by S(**i**). The term *statement* is used for the program assignment statement S and the term *instance* for each of the particular assignment statements that S generates for different iterations of **nest(S)**.

Consider now two (not necessarily distinct) assignment statements S and T in the program. They determine three disjoint nests: the *common nest* **L** of loops containing both S and T, the nest **L**$_S$ of loops containing S but not T, and the nest **L**$_T$ of loops containing T but not S. Let there be e loops in **L**, m loops in **L** and **L**$_S$, and n loops all together in **L**, **L**$_S$, and **L**$_T$. Label these loops L_1, L_2,..., L_n in such a way that

$$
\begin{aligned}
\mathbf{L} &= (L_1, L_2,..., L_e) \\
\mathbf{L}_S &= (L_{e+1}, L_{e+2},..., L_m) \\
\mathbf{L}_T &= (L_{m+1}, L_{m+2},..., L_n).
\end{aligned}
$$

(See Example 2.3.3.) Let I_k denote the index variable, p_k the lower limit, and q_k the upper limit of L_k, (k = 1, 2,..., n). Then the indexes **I**, **I**$_S$, **I**$_T$ of the nests **L**, **L**$_S$, **L**$_T$, respectively, are given by

$$
\begin{aligned}
\mathbf{I} &= (I_1, I_2,..., I_e) \\
\mathbf{I}_S &= (I_{e+1}, I_{e+2},..., I_m) \\
\mathbf{I}_T &= (I_{m+1}, I_{m+2},..., I_n).
\end{aligned}
$$

The lower and upper limits of the nests have similar expressions. Now **nest(S)** = (**L**, **L**$_S$) and **nest(T)** = (**L**, **L**$_T$), where (,) denotes concatenation. There are m loops in **nest(S)** and (n − m + e) loops in **nest(T)**. The index of **nest(S)** is (**I**, **I**$_S$) and the index of **nest(T)** is (**I**, **I**$_T$). We denote an arbitrary iteration of **nest(S)** by (**i**, **i**$_S$) where **i** = (i_1, i_2,..., i_e) is an iteration of **L** and **i**$_S$ = (i_{e+1}, i_{e+2},..., i_m) an iteration of **L**$_S$, and an arbitrary iteration of **nest(T)** by (**j**, **j**$_T$)

where $\mathbf{j} = (j_1, j_2,..., j_e)$ and $\mathbf{j}_T = (j_{m+1}, j_{m+2},..., j_n)$ are iterations of L and L_T, respectively. This notation that clearly separates the three nests L, L_S, L_T is helpful in the specification of execution ordering of statement instances and formulation of the dependence problem.

We use $S < T$ to denote that S precedes T lexically in the program. It is easy to see then that $\leq$ is a total order on the set of assignment statements. The conditions under which an instance of S precedes an instance of T in the serial execution of the program are given below. Note that these conditions involve only iterations of the common nest L.

Lemma 2.3.1. Let S, T denote two assignment statements in the program. An instance $S(\mathbf{i}, \mathbf{i}_S)$ of S is executed before an instance $T(\mathbf{j}, \mathbf{j}_T)$ of T in the serial execution of the program, iff

$$\mathbf{i} \leq \mathbf{j} \quad \text{for the case } S < T,$$

or

$$\mathbf{i} < \mathbf{j} \quad \text{for the case } T \leq S.$$

PROOF. In the serial execution of the program, all instances of all statements are executed one by one in a definite order. We are given an iteration $(\mathbf{i}, \mathbf{i}_S)$ of $\mathbf{nest}(S) = (L, L_S)$ and an iteration $(\mathbf{j}, \mathbf{j}_T)$ of $\mathbf{nest}(T) = (L, L_T)$ and are considering the execution ordering of the instances $S(\mathbf{i}, \mathbf{i}_S)$ and $T(\mathbf{j}, \mathbf{j}_T)$. There are three cases:

Case 1. $S < T$.

If $\mathbf{i} < \mathbf{j}$, then the iteration $I = \mathbf{i}$ of the common nest L is executed before the iteration $I = \mathbf{j}$, and hence $S(\mathbf{i}, \mathbf{i}_S)$ is executed before $T(\mathbf{j}, \mathbf{j}_T)$. If $\mathbf{j} < \mathbf{i}$, then what we just said implies that $T(\mathbf{j}, \mathbf{j}_T)$ is executed before $S(\mathbf{i}, \mathbf{i}_S)$. Now let $\mathbf{i} = \mathbf{j}$. Since $S < T$, the nest L_S appears before the nest L_T in the program. In a given iteration $\mathbf{i}$ of the common nest, any instance $S(\mathbf{i}, \mathbf{i}_S)$ of S will be executed before any instance $T(\mathbf{i}, \mathbf{j}_T)$ of T. Thus, $S(\mathbf{i}, \mathbf{i}_S)$ is executed before $T(\mathbf{j}, \mathbf{j}_T)$ iff $\mathbf{i} \leq \mathbf{j}$.

Case 2. $T < S$.

It follows from Case (1) that $T(\mathbf{j}, \mathbf{j}_T)$ is executed before $S(\mathbf{i}, \mathbf{i}_S)$ iff $\mathbf{j} \le \mathbf{i}$. In other words, $S(\mathbf{i}, \mathbf{i}_S)$ is executed before $T(\mathbf{j}, \mathbf{j}_T)$ iff $\mathbf{i} < \mathbf{j}$.

Case 3. $S = T$.

The nests $\mathbf{L}_S$ and $\mathbf{L}_T$ are empty, and the instances $S(\mathbf{i}, \mathbf{i}_S)$, $T(\mathbf{j}, \mathbf{j}_T)$ are simply $S(\mathbf{i})$, $S(\mathbf{j})$. If $\mathbf{i} < \mathbf{j}$, then $S(\mathbf{i})$ is executed before $S(\mathbf{j})$. If $\mathbf{j} < \mathbf{i}$, the opposite is true. If $\mathbf{i} = \mathbf{j}$, then the instances are identical, and one cannot be executed before the other. Thus $S(\mathbf{i})$ is executed before $S(\mathbf{j})$ iff $\mathbf{i} < \mathbf{j}$.   ◆

Example 2.3.1. The perfect nest of two loops

L: **do** $I_1 = 1, 100$
                do $I_2 = 1, 50$
                        $\vdots$
S: $A(I_1, I_2) = B(I_1) * C(3*I_1 + 1, I_2) - z + 5$
                        $\vdots$
                enddo
        enddo

has 5,000 iterations. If **L** is executed serially, these iterations must come in the lexicographic order: $(I_1, I_2) = (1, 1), (1, 2),..., (1, 50)$, $(2, 1), (2, 2),..., (2, 50),..., (100, 1), (100, 2),..., (100, 50)$. An iteration (i_1, i_2) precedes an iteration (j_1, j_2) iff $(i_1, i_2) < (j_1, j_2)$. If $i_1 < j_1$ this happens, since then we have $(i_1, i_2) <_1 (j_1, j_2)$, and the values of i_2, j_2 are immaterial. When the iteration of the outer loop is fixed, i_2 must be less than j_2 (and hence $(i_1, i_2) <_2 (j_1, j_2)$) to ensure that iteration (i_1, i_2) comes before iteration (j_1, j_2).

For the statement S we have $\text{nest}(S) = \mathbf{L}$. The sets of output and input variables of S are given by

$$OUT(S) \equiv OUT\big(S(I_1, I_2)\big) = \big\{A(I_1, I_2)\big\}$$
$$IN(S) \equiv IN\big(S(I_1, I_2)\big) = \big\{B(I_1), C(3*I_1 + 1, I_2), z\big\}.$$

For the instance $S(2, 3)$ of S, these sets are

$$OUT(S(2, 3)) = \{A(2, 3)\}$$
and $$IN(S(2, 3)) = \{B(2), C(7, 3), z\}.$$

Example 2.3.2. Consider a program of the form

$$
\begin{aligned}
&L_1: &&\textbf{do } I_1 = 1, 2 \\
&L_2: &&\quad \textbf{do } I_2 = 1, 2 \\
&L_3: &&\quad\quad \textbf{do } I_3 = 1, 2 \\
& && \quad\quad\quad S(I_1, I_2, I_3) \\
& && \quad\quad \textbf{enddo} \\
&L_4: &&\quad\quad \textbf{do } I_4 = 1, 2 \\
& && \quad\quad\quad T(I_1, I_2, I_4) \\
& && \quad\quad \textbf{enddo} \\
& && \quad \textbf{enddo} \\
& && \textbf{enddo}
\end{aligned}
$$

where S denotes a statement in loop L_3 and T a statement in loop L_4. We have $S < T$, $e = 2$, $m = 3$, and $n = 4$. The number of loops containing both S and T is $e = 2$, containing S but not T is $m - e = 1$, and containing T but not S is $n - m = 1$. The nest of loops containing both S and T is $L = (L_1, L_2)$, containing S but not T is $L_S = (L_3)$, and containing T but not S is $L_T = (L_4)$. Thus, the nest of all loops containing S is $\textbf{nest}(S) = (L_1, L_2, L_3)$, and the nest of all loops containing T is $\textbf{nest}(T) = (L_1, L_2, L_4)$. There are eight instances of S, eight instances of T, and in the serial execution of the program they are executed in the following order (left to right, top to bottom):

$$
\begin{aligned}
&S(1, 1, 1), \ S(1, 1, 2), \ T(1, 1, 1), \ T(1, 1, 2), \\
&S(1, 2, 1), \ S(1, 2, 2), \ T(1, 2, 1), \ T(1, 2, 2), \\
&S(2, 1, 1), \ S(2, 1, 2), \ T(2, 1, 1), \ T(2, 1, 2), \\
&S(2, 2, 1), \ S(2, 2, 2), \ T(2, 2, 1), \ T(2, 2, 2).
\end{aligned}
$$

Each row represents an iteration of the common nest L. The order of iterations of L controls the execution ordering of instances of S and T. In a given iteration (i_1, i_2) of L, any instance $S(i_1, i_2, i_3)$ of S will precede any instance $T(i_1, i_2, j_4)$ of T. An arbitrary instance $S(i_1, i_2, i_3)$ of S precedes an arbitrary instance $T(j_1, j_2, j_4)$ of T iff $(i_1, i_2) \leq (j_1, j_2)$. On the other hand, $T(j_1, j_2, j_4)$ precedes $S(i_1, i_2, i_3)$ iff strictly $(j_1, j_2) < (i_1, i_2)$. This is because statement T comes lexically after statement S in the program.

Example 2.3.3. To further clarify our notation, here we show a program with two statements S and T such that $S < T$.

$$L_1: \qquad \textbf{do } I_1 = p_1, q_1$$
$$\vdots \qquad\qquad \vdots$$
$$L_e: \qquad \textbf{do } I_e = p_e, q_e$$
$$L_{e+1}: \qquad\quad \textbf{do } I_{e+1} = p_{e+1}, q_{e+1}$$
$$\vdots \qquad\qquad\qquad \vdots$$
$$L_m: \qquad\qquad \textbf{do } I_m = p_m, q_m$$

$$S(I_1,..., I_e, I_{e+1},..., I_m)$$

$$\textbf{enddo}$$
$$\vdots$$
$$\textbf{enddo}$$
$$L_{m+1}: \qquad \textbf{do } I_{m+1} = p_{m+1}, q_{m+1}$$
$$\vdots \qquad\qquad \vdots$$
$$L_n: \qquad\quad \textbf{do } I_n = p_n, q_n$$

$$T(I_1,..., I_e, I_{m+1},..., I_n)$$

$$\textbf{enddo}$$
$$\vdots$$
$$\textbf{enddo}$$
$$\textbf{enddo}$$
$$\vdots$$
$$\textbf{enddo}$$

CHAPTER 3

DEPENDENCE

We continue to use the notation developed in Section 2.3. The program under consideration is a loop that may contain (assignment) statements and more loops. Two statements S and T are chosen arbitrarily in the program. They define a number of nests: the common nest L consisting of loops containing both S and T, the nest L_S of loops containing S but not T, the nest L_T of loops containing T but not S, $nest(S) = (L, L_S)$ consisting of all loops containing S, and $nest(T) = (L, L_T)$ consisting of all loops containing T. The indexes of the nests L, L_S, L_T are denoted by I, I_S, I_T, respectively, so that the indexes of $nest(S)$ and $nest(T)$ are (I, I_S) and (I, I_T). The fundamental dependence concepts are explained in the first section of this chapter and the results underlying dependence tests are studied in the second.

27

3.1. DEPENDENCE CONCEPTS

Statement T *depends* on statement S (in symbols, S δ T) if there exist an instance S´ of S, an instance T´ of T, and a memory location M, such that

1. Both S´ and T´ reference M, and at least one of those references is a write;
2. In the serial execution of the program, S´ is executed before T´; and
3. In the same execution, M is not written between the time S´ finishes and the time T´ starts.

Thus there are three types of dependence based upon the types of the two references to M. Statement T is

flow-dependent on S, if S´ writes M and then T´ reads it;
anti-dependent on S, if S´ reads M and then T´ writes it;
output-dependent on S, if S´ writes M and then T´ writes it again.

We use S δ^f T to denote flow-dependence, S δ^a T for anti-dependence, and S δ^o T for output dependence. (The notation usually seen in the literature uses δ, $\bar{\delta}$, δ^o for flow, anti, and output dependences, respectively.)

The concept of a fourth type of relationship, created when S´ and T´ both read M, may be useful sometimes, but we will not consider it. In case of flow-dependence, the value stored in M by S´ is the value actually used by T´. For anti-dependence, S´ uses the value stored in M before it is changed by T´. For output-dependence, T´ must store in M after S´ stores in M.

The next step is to analyze these concepts at the level of variables and iterations. The following is simply a restatement of the definition of dependence: Statement T *depends* on statement S if there exist a variable x of S, a variable y of T, an iteration (i, i_S) of **nest**(S), and an iteration (j, j_T) of **nest**(T), such that

1. At least one of x, y is the output variable of its statement;

2. x in iteration (i, i_S) and y in iteration (j, j_T) represent the same memory location M;

3. In the serial execution of the program, the instance $S(i, i_S)$ of S is executed before the instance $T(j, j_T)$ of T; and

4. In the same execution, M is not written between the time $S(i, i_S)$ finishes and the time $T(j, j_T)$ starts.

(The instances $S(i, i_S)$ and $T(j, j_T)$ in this definition correspond to S´ and T´ in the previous one.) If two variables x, y and two iterations (i, i_S), (j, j_T) satisfy these four conditions, then we say that the pair (x, y) *causes a dependence* of T on S, and that the iteration pair $((i, i_S), (j, j_T))$ is *associated* with the dependence caused by (x, y).

The three types of dependence correspond to the three possible combinations of output and input variables. The dependence caused by a pair of variables (x, y) is a

flow-dependence, if $x \in OUT(S)$ and $y \in IN(T)$;
anti-dependence, if $x \in IN(S)$ and $y \in OUT(T)$;
output-dependence, if $x \in OUT(S)$ and $y \in OUT(T)$.

Thus, T is dependent on S if there is at least one pair of variables (x, y) causing a dependece (of any type) of T on S. Also, T is flow-dependent on S if there is at least one input variable y of T, such that (x, y), where $x \in OUT(S)$, causes a dependence of T on S; and so on.

By Lemma 2.3.1, condition 3 in the previous paragraph can be satisfied in two possible ways: either iteration i of nest L precedes iteration j, or the two iterations are identical. If $i < j$, the instance $S(i, i_S)$ of S will be executed before the instance $T(j, j_T)$ of T, irrespectively of the lexical positions of the two statements. In the case $i = j$, however, $S(i, i_S)$ will be executed before $T(j, j_T)$ iff S precedes T lexically in the program. In order that the relation $i < j$ may hold, we must have $i <_u j$ for exactly one member u of the set $\{1, 2, ..., e\}$. (Remember that i, j are iterations of the common nest L that has e loops.) Also, the notation $i <_{e+1} j$ means $i = j$. We say that a pair of variables (x, y) *causes a dependence* of T on S at a *level* u, if (x, y) causes a dependence and there is an associated iteration pair $((i, i_S), (j, j_T))$ with $i <_u j$. The possible levels are 1, 2,..., e, e + 1 for S < T, and 1, 2,..., e for T ≤ S. The same variables *cause* a *dependence* at a *depth* DEP, if they cause a dependence at a level u ≥ DEP. The possible depths are 1, 2,..., e, e + 1 for S < T, and 1, 2,..., e for T ≤ S. Note that dependence at a depth DEP implies dependence at each of the depths 1, 2,..., DEP − 1. The level information may not always be enough—we may want to know more about the iteration pairs associated with a dependence. A pair of variables (x, y) *causes* a *dependence* of T on S with a *direction vector* $s = (s_1, s_2,..., s_e)$, if (x, y) causes a dependence and there is an associated iteration pair $((i, i_S), (j, j_T))$ such that s is the direction vector of (i, j), i.e.,

$$sig(j_k - i_k) = s_k \quad \text{for } 1 \le k \le e.$$

Note that any direction vector in this context must satisfy $s \ge 0$ for S < T, and $s > 0$ for the case T ≤ S, (Lemma 2.2.2). Also, having dependence at a level u is same as having dependence with a direction vector of the form (0,..., 0, 1, *,..., *) with (u − 1) zeros in front (Lemma 2.2.2). Statement T *depends* on statement S at a *level* u , at a *depth* DEP, or with a *direction vector* s, if there is a variable x of S and a variable y of T, such that (x, y) causes a dependence of T on S at level u, at depth DEP, or with direction vector s, respectively.

If variables x, y cause a dependence of T on S and an associated iteration pair is $((i, i_S), (j, j_T))$, then the distance vector of (i, j), namely the vector

$$(j_1 - i_1, j_2 - i_2,..., j_e - i_e),$$

is called a *distance vector* of this dependence. If each associated pair of iterations yields the same distance vector, then the dependence caused by (x, y) has a *constant* distance vector. We say that T depends on S with a constant distance vector, if every pair of variables (x, y) that causes a dependence has the same constant distance vector. Given a distance vector, we can compute the corresponding direction vector; and given a direction vector, we can compute the corresponding level. However, there could be many possible direction vectors for a given level and many possible distance vectors for a given direction vector.

The type (flow, anti, output) of a dependence can be combined with the ideas of level, depth, direction and distance vectors in an obvious way. Thus, for instance, we may talk about variables (x, y) causing a flow-dependence of T on S at a level u and with a certain constant distance vector. Also, the meaning is clear when we say, for example, that T is output-dependent on S with a direction vector s. The level may be shown as a subscript: $S \, \delta_u^f \, T$ would mean that T is flow-dependent on S at a level u, and similar notation may be used for the other two types of dependence. A direction vector may also be included in the notation. Thus, to specify that T is flow-dependent on S at a level u and with a direction vector s, we will write $S \, \delta_u^f(s) \, T$.

Example 3.1.1. Consider the single loop

```
L:          do I = 3, 100
    S:          A(2*I) = B(I) + 2
    T:          C(I) = D(I) + A(2*I + 1) + A(2*I - 4) + A(I)
            enddo
```

The nests L_S and L_T are empty, and the nests L, **nest**(S), **nest**(T) are all same as L. We take the output variable A(2I) of S as the variable x in the above discussion; the four input variables of T would take turns to be the variable y. The output variable A(2I) of S and the input variable D(I) of T cannot cause a flow-dependence of T on S, since they would never represent the same memory location. (The arrays A and D are different.) Although the variable A(2I) and the variable A(2I + 1) represent elements of the same array, they still cannot cause a flow-dependence for the same reason. The location A(2i) represented by A(2I) in any iteration I = i will never be the same as the location A(2j + 1) represented by

A(2I + 1) in any iteration I = j, since the subscripts 2i and (2j + 1) are different for all values of i, j.

It is easy to see that the variables A(2I) and A(2I − 4) do cause a flow-dependence of T on S. The iterations I = 3 and I = 5 are such that

1. The memory location represented by the variable A(2I) in iteration I = 3 is same as the location represented by A(2I − 4) in iteration I = 5, since A(2∗3) and A(2∗5 − 4) are both A(6);

2. The instance S(3) is executed before the instance T(5) in the serial execution of the program; and

3. The value stored in A(6) by S(3) is used by T(5) in the same execution.

In fact, the complete set of associated iteration pairs is

$$\{(i, j): j = i + 2, \ 3 \le i \le 98\}.$$

For each pair (i, j) in this set, the direction (vector) is 1 and the distance (vector) is 2, since i < j and j − i = 2, respectively. Thus, the flow-dependence of T on S caused by the variables A(2I) and A(2I − 4) has a constant direction 1 and a constant distance 2.

Now compare the variables A(2I) of S and A(I) of T. It turns out that they too cause a flow-dependence of T on S. The set of associated iteration pairs is

$$\{(i, j): j = 2i, \ 3 \le i \le 50\}.$$

For an (i, j) in this set, the direction is 1 since i < j, and the distance is j − i = i. Thus, this flow-dependence has a constant direction of 1, but a variable distance that ranges from 3 to 50.

Summarizing the above discussion, we can say that statement T is flow-dependent on statement S, with a constant direction of 1, a minimum distance of 2, and a maximum distance of 50.

Example 3.1.2. The concepts of dependence at a level and at a depth can be understood by studying the loop nest:

```
do I₁ = 1, 100
   do I₂ = 1, 50
S:       A(I₁, I₂) = A(I₁ − 3, I₂) + A(I₁, I₂ − 2) − A(I₁ − 1, I₂ + 1)
   enddo
enddo
```

The output variable of S and any of the three input variables cause a flow-dependence of S on itself. Consider first $A(I_1, I_2)$ and $A(I_1 - 3, I_2)$. The element $A(i_1, i_2)$ represented by $A(I_1, I_2)$ in an iteration $(I_1, I_2) = (i_1, i_2)$, and the element $A(j_1 - 3, j_2)$ represented by $A(I_1 - 3, I_2)$ in an iteration $(I_1, I_2) = (j_1, j_2)$ would be the same, iff

$$i_1 = j_1 - 3 \quad \text{and} \quad i_2 = j_2.$$

There are, of course, many iteration pairs (i_1, i_2), (j_1, j_2) of the nest that satisfy these equations, e.g., (1, 2) and (4, 2), (12, 3) and (15, 3), and so on. For each such pair we have $i_1 < j_1$, so that $(i_1, i_2) <_1 (j_1, j_2)$. Thus, these two variables cause a flow-dependence at level 1, and hence at depth 1. Also, this dependence has a constant direction vector of (1, 0) and a constant distance vector of (3, 0). Similarly, it can be shown that the variables $A(I_1, I_2)$ and $A(I_1, I_2 - 2)$ cause a flow-dependence of S on itself at level 2 with direction vector (0, 1) and distance vector (0, 2). Dependence at level 2 implies dependence at depth 1 and at depth 2. Again, the variables $A(I_1, I_2)$ and $A(I_1 - 1, I_2 + 1)$ cause a flow-dependence at level 1 with direction vector (1, −1) and distance vector (1, −1). Ignoring particular variables, we could say that S is flow-dependent on itself at levels 1, 2 (and hence at depths 1, 2). For the dependence at level 1, the direction vectors are (1, 0), (1, −1) and the distance vectors are (3, 0), (1, −1). The dependence at level 2 has a direction vector of (0, 1) and a distance vector of (0, 2).

If x is the output variable of S and y an input variable of T, then the pair (x, y) may cause the flow-dependence S δ^f T, and the opposite pair (y, x) may cause the anti-dependence T δ^a S. If x and y are the output variables of S and T respectively, the pair (x, y) may cause the output-dependence S δ^o T and the pair (y, x) the output-dependence T δ^o S.

Statement T is *indirectly dependent* on statement S, if there are statements $S_1, S_2,..., S_l$ such that

$$S \delta S_1, \quad S_1 \delta S_2,..., \quad S_{l-1} \delta S_l, \quad S_l \delta T$$

(i.e., if S, S_1, S_2,..., S_l, T form a chain with respect to the relation δ). Dependence obviously implies indirect dependence. Usually, by the *dependence graph* of the program we mean the graph of the relation δ, i.e., it is a digraph where the nodes correspond to the (assignment) statements in the program, and there is an arc from a node S to a node T iff S δ T. Each arc may be labeled with information about type, levels, direction vectors, etc. Sometimes, we consider the *level graphs*: the graphs of the relations δ_1, δ_2, etc. In a general sense, the graph of any of the dependence relations defined in this section is a dependence graph of the program and may serve some useful purpose.

It is clear that one may write down many identities involving the various dependence relations we have defined. For example,

1. $\delta = \delta^f \cup \delta^a \cup \delta^o$;
2. $\delta_k = \delta_k^f \cup \delta_k^a \cup \delta_k^o$;

3. The relation of dependence at depth DEP is the union of the relations δ_k for each possible level $k \geq$ DEP;

4. The relation of indirect dependence is the transitive closure of the relation δ;

and so on. We leave it to the reader to complete this list.

Example 3.1.3. Consider

$$
\begin{array}{ll}
& \textbf{do } I = 8, 74 \\
S: & B(I) = A(I) + 3 \\
T: & A(I - 1) = C(2*I + 5) - 1 \\
U: & A(I) = 2 \\
& \textbf{enddo}
\end{array}
$$

In the serial execution of the program, the instances come as follows:

S(8):	B(8)	= A(8) + 3
T(8):	A(7)	= C(21) − 1
U(8):	A(8)	= 2
S(9):	B(9)	= A(9) + 3
T(9):	A(8)	= C(23) − 1
U(9):	A(9)	= 2
S(10):	B(10)	= A(10) + 3
T(10):	A(9)	= C(25) − 1

$$\vdots$$

The instances S(8), U(8), and T(9) all reference the memory location A(8), but the value used by S(8) is the one that existed before the loop started and not the value computed by U(8) or T(9). The same pattern is repeated throughout the loop. The input variable A(I) of S and the output variable A(I) of U cause statement U to be anti-dependent on statement S, since there is an iteration I = 8, such that

   1. Both variables in that iteration reference the same memory location A(8);

   2. The instance S(8) is executed before the instance U(8) in the serial execution of the program; and

   3. In the same execution, the location A(8) is not written between the time S(8) finishes and the time U(8) starts.

(We could take any other iteration of the loop to satisfy these conditions.) Note that the input variable A(I) of S and the output variable A(I − 1) of T do not cause T to be anti-dependent on S. This is because the last condition in the definition of dependence no longer holds in this case: for any i in 8 ≤ i ≤ 74, between the use of A(i) by the instance S(i) of S and the definition of A(i) by the instance T(i + 1) of T, there is the definition of A(i) by the instance U(i) of U. It is easy to see, however, that T is output-dependent on U, so that T is indirectly dependent on S.

3.2. THE DEPENDENCE PROBLEM

To test if a statement T depends on a statement S in a certain specified way, one must compare their variable lists and consider variable pairs that are candidates to cause dependence. The (input or output) nature of the variables under consideration determines the type of the potential dependence; e.g., when the output variable of S is being considered along with an input variable of T, we are testing for possible flow-dependence of T on S. For a given pair of variables, it may not always be possible to compute the complete set of associated iteration pairs. However, in many cases, there are necessary conditions for the existence of dependence at a certain level or with a certain direction vector. Testing such conditions, we are able to decide when a dependence of a certain kind *does not* exist, even if the set of associated iteration pairs cannot be found. Comparing two occurrences of the same scalar is easy; we concentrate here on array elements. Merely checking the names of arrays would usually yield a primitive and highly inaccurate graph—to improve accuracy, subscripts must also be compared after a match in names has been found. Theorem 3.2.1 is the fundamental theorem of dependence analysis. It characterizes an iteration pair for a given dependence problem (at a level or with a direction vector) as a solution to a system of equations and inequalities; the existence of a solution means that the specified dependence also exists. Recall from Section 2.3 that the index of nest(S) is $(\mathbf{I}, \mathbf{I}_S) = (I_1, I_2,..., I_e, I_{e+1},..., I_m)$, the index of nest(T) is $(\mathbf{I}, \mathbf{I}_T) = (I_1, I_2,...., I_e, I_{m+1}, I_{m+2},..., I_n)$, and that the lower and upper limits of the I_k-loop are p_k, q_k, respectively, $1 \le k \le n$.

From now on, when testing for dependence, we will drop the last requirement in the definition as stated in the previous section, namely that the memory location M be not written between the time the instance $S(\mathbf{i}, \mathbf{i}_S)$ of S finishes and the time the instance $T(\mathbf{j}, \mathbf{j}_T)$ of T starts. This may sometimes introduce a false dependence of T on S. But when that happens, as shown in Example 3.1.3, T would be *indirectly* dependent on S anyway, and the fact that is important to an optimizing compiler is whether or not there is a *path* from S to T in the dependence graph. Sentences like " ... causes a dependence iff ... ," and " ... there is dependence only if ... ," used below should be interpreted in the light of this understanding.

Theorem 3.2.1. Let A denote an array of dimension DIM, and

$$f_r\colon \mathbf{Z}^m \to \mathbf{Z} \quad \text{and} \quad g_r\colon \mathbf{Z}^{n-m+e} \to \mathbf{Z}, \qquad (1 \le r \le \text{DIM}),$$

two sets of functions. Let x denote a variable of S and y a variable of T, such that at least one of x, y is the output variable of its statement and

$$x = A\big(f_1(\mathbf{I}, \mathbf{I}_S), f_2(\mathbf{I}, \mathbf{I}_S),..., f_{\text{DIM}}(\mathbf{I}, \mathbf{I}_S)\big)$$
$$y = A\big(g_1(\mathbf{I}, \mathbf{I}_T), g_2(\mathbf{I}, \mathbf{I}_T),..., g_{\text{DIM}}(\mathbf{I}, \mathbf{I}_T)\big).$$

Then (x, y) causes a dependence of T on S with a direction vector s = $(s_1, s_2,..., s_e)$, iff there is an integer solution to the system of DIM equations

$$f_r(i_1, i_2,..., i_e, i_{e+1},..., i_m) = g_r(j_1, j_2,...., j_e, j_{m+1}, j_{m+2},..., j_n),$$

$$(1 \le r \le \text{DIM}), \qquad (1)$$

satisfying the conditions:

$$p_k \le i_k \le q_k, \qquad (1 \le k \le m);$$
$$p_k \le j_k \le q_k, \qquad (1 \le k \le e \text{ and } m+1 \le k \le n); \qquad (2)$$

and

$$i_k - j_k \begin{cases} < 0 & \text{if } s_k = 1 \\ = 0 & \text{if } s_k = 0 \\ > 0 & \text{if } s_k = -1 \end{cases}$$

$$(1 \le k \le e). \qquad (3)$$

There are $N = n + e - \Omega$ independent integer variables in (1), where Ω is the number of zeros in the direction vector s. (We must have $s \ge 0$ for the case $S < T$ and $s > 0$ for the case $T \le S$.)

PROOF. Consider first the 'only if' part. Suppose the variables x, y cause S δ T. Then there is an iteration $(i_1, i_2,..., i_e, i_{e+1},..., i_m)$ of **nest**(S) and an iteration $(j_1, j_2,....., j_e, j_{m+1}, j_{m+2},..., j_n)$ of **nest**(T) that satisfy the definition of dependence given in Section 3.1. In order to make the memory location represented by x in iteration $(i_1, i_2,..., i_e, i_{e+1},..., i_m)$ identical to the location represented by y in iteration $(j_1, j_2,....., j_e, j_{m+1}, j_{m+2},..., j_n)$, each pair of corresponding subscripts of x, y in the respective iterations must be equal. This means there must be an integer solution to the system of equations (1). Since i_1, j_1 are values of the index variable I_1, they must satisfy the limits of I_1, and similarly for the other variables. This explains the conditions (2). Finally, conditions (3) simply say that the iteration pair has the given direction vector **s**. The direction vector must be $\geq$ **0** for the case S < T, and > **0** for the case T $\leq$ S to make sure that the instance S$(i_1, i_2,..., i_e, i_{e+1},..., i_m)$ is executed before the instance T$(j_1, j_2,....., j_e, j_{m+1}, j_{m+2},..., j_n)$ in the serial execution of the program.

For the 'if' part, trace the steps backwards (see the comments at the beginning of the section).   ♦

If only dependence at a given level is to be tested, the conditions are simpler:

Corollary. In the notation of the above theorem, (x, y) causes a dependence of T on S at a level u, iff there is an integer solution to the system of DIM equations

$$f_r(i_1, i_2,..., i_e, i_{e+1},..., i_m) = g_r(i_1, i_2,..., i_{u-1}, j_u,..., j_e, j_{m+1},..., j_n),$$

$$(1 \leq r \leq \text{DIM}), \ (1)$$

in $N = (n + e - u + 1)$ variables, subject to the conditions:

$$p_k \leq i_k \leq q_k, \quad (1 \leq k \leq m);$$
$$p_k \leq j_k \leq q_k, \quad (u \leq k \leq e \text{ and } m + 1 \leq k \leq n); \quad (2)$$

and

$$i_u < j_u, \qquad \text{if } 1 \le u \le e. \qquad (3)$$

(The possible levels are $u = 1, 2,..., e + 1$ for the case $S < T$, and $u = 1, 2,..., e$ for the case $T \le S$.)

PROOF. The corollary follows immediately from the theorem, since dependence at a level u means dependence with a direction vector of the form $(0, 0,..., 0, 1, *,..., *)$ with $(u - 1)$ zeros in front. We substitute i_1 for j_1, i_2 for j_2,..., i_{u-1} for j_{u-1} to simplify the equations. ♦

We assume now that all functions are linear and state the linear dependence problem. All coefficients given below are integer constants.

In the common nest $\mathbf{L}$ with index $\mathbf{I} = (I_1, I_2,..., I_e)$, let the lower limit p_k and upper limit q_k of I_k be given by.

$$p_k = p_{k0} + p_{k1}I_1 + p_{k2} I_2 + \cdots + p_{k,k-1}I_{k-1}$$
$$q_k = q_{k0} + q_{k1}I_1 + q_{k2} I_2 + \cdots + q_{k,k-1}I_{k-1}, \qquad (1 \le k \le e).$$

In the nest $\mathbf{L_S}$ with index $\mathbf{I_S} = (I_{e+1}, I_{e+2},..., I_m)$, let the lower and upper limits p_k, q_k of I_k be given by

$$p_k = p_{k0} + p_{k1}I_1 + \cdots + p_{ke}I_e + p_{k,e+1}I_{e+1} + \cdots + p_{k,k-1}I_{k-1}$$
$$q_k = q_{k0} + q_{k1}I_1 + \cdots + q_{ke}I_e + q_{k,e+1}I_{e+1} + \cdots + q_{k,k-1}I_{k-1},$$
$$(e + 1 \le k \le m).$$

In the nest $\mathbf{L_T}$ with index $\mathbf{I_T} = (I_{m+1}, I_{m+2},..., I_n)$, let the lower and upper limits p_k, q_k of I_k be given by

$$p_k = p_{k0} + p_{k1}I_1 + \cdots + p_{ke}I_e + p_{k,m+1}I_{m+1} + \cdots + p_{k,k-1}I_{k-1}$$
$$q_k = q_{k0} + q_{k1}I_1 + \cdots + q_{ke}I_e + q_{k,m+1}I_{m+1} + \cdots + q_{k,k-1}I_{k-1},$$
$$(m + 1 \le k \le n).$$

The important thing to remember here is that the limits in nest $\mathbf{L}_S$ do not depend on the index variables in nest $\mathbf{L}_T$, and vice versa.

Assume that the subscript functions of the variables

$$x = A\big(f_1(\mathbf{I}, \mathbf{I}_S), f_2(\mathbf{I}, \mathbf{I}_S),..., f_{DIM}(\mathbf{I}, \mathbf{I}_S)\big)$$
$$y = A\big(g_1(\mathbf{I}, \mathbf{I}_T), g_2(\mathbf{I}, \mathbf{I}_T),..., g_{DIM}(\mathbf{I}, \mathbf{I}_T)\big).$$

of statements S and T have the following forms:

$$f_r(\mathbf{I}, \mathbf{I}_S) = a_{r0} + a_{r1}i_1 + \cdots + a_{re}i_e + a_{r,e+1}i_{e+1} + \cdots + a_{rm}i_m$$
$$g_r(\mathbf{I}, \mathbf{I}_T) = b_{r0} + b_{r1}i_1 + \cdots + b_{re}i_e + b_{r,m+1}i_{m+1} + \cdots + b_{rn}i_n,$$

$$(1 \leq r \leq DIM).$$

Theorem 3.2.2. (Linear Version of Theorem 3.2.1.)

The variables x of statement S and y of statement T cause a dependence of T on S with a direction vector $\mathbf{s} = (s_1, s_2,..., s_e)$, iff there is an integer solution to the system of DIM equations

$$(a_{r1}i_1 - b_{r1}j_1) + \cdots + (a_{re}i_e - b_{re}j_e) + a_{r,e+1}i_{e+1} + a_{rm}i_m - b_{r,m+1}j_{m+1}$$
$$- \cdots - b_{rn}j_n$$
$$= b_{r0} - a_{r0}, \qquad (1 \leq r \leq DIM),$$

satisfying the conditions:

$$p_{k0} + p_{k1}i_1 + \cdots + p_{k,k-1}i_{k-1} \leq i_k \leq q_{k0} + q_{k1}i_1 + \cdots + q_{k,k-1}i_{k-1},$$
$$(1 \leq k \leq m);$$

$$p_{k0} + p_{k1}j_1 + \cdots + p_{k,k-1}j_{k-1} \leq j_k \leq q_{k0} + q_{k1}j_1 + \cdots + q_{k,k-1}j_{k-1},$$
$$(1 \leq k \leq e);$$

$$p_{k0} + p_{k1}j_1 + \cdots + p_{ke}j_e + p_{k,m+1}j_{m+1} + \cdots + p_{k,k-1}j_{k-1}$$
$$\leq j_k$$
$$\leq q_{k0} + q_{k1}j_1 + \cdots + q_{ke}j_e + q_{k,m+1}j_{m+1} + \cdots + q_{k,k-1}j_{k-1},$$
$$(m + 1 \leq k \leq n);$$

and

$$i_k - j_k \begin{cases} < 0 & \text{if } s_k = 1 \\ = 0 & \text{if } s_k = 0 \\ > 0 & \text{if } s_k = -1 \end{cases}$$

$$(1 \le k \le e).$$

The number of integer variables in the system is $N = n + e - \Omega$, where Ω is the number of zeros in s. (We must have $s \ge 0$ for the case $S < T$ and $s > 0$ for the case $T \le S$.)

Corollary 1. (Linear Version of Corollary to Theorem 3.2.1.)

The variables x, y cause a dependence of statement T on statement S at a level u, iff there is an integer solution to the system of DIM equations

$$(a_{r1} - b_{r1})i_1 + \cdots + (a_{r,u-1} - b_{r,u-1})i_{u-1} + (a_{ru}i_u - b_{ru}j_u) + \cdots$$
$$+ (a_{re}i_e - b_{re}j_e) + a_{r,e+1}i_{e+1} + a_{rm}i_m - b_{r,m+1}j_{m+1} - \cdots - b_{rm}j_n$$

$$= b_{r0} - a_{r0}, \qquad (1 \le r \le DIM),$$

in $N = (n + e - u + 1)$ variables, satisfying the conditions:

$$p_{k0} + p_{k1}i_1 + \cdots + p_{k,k-1}i_{k-1} \le i_k \le q_{k0} + q_{k1}i_1 + \cdots + q_{k,k-1}i_{k-1},$$
$$(1 \le k \le m);$$

$$p_{k0} + p_{k1}i_1 + \cdots + p_{k,u-1}i_{u-1} + p_{ku}j_u + \cdots + p_{k,k-1}j_{k-1}$$
$$\le j_k$$
$$\le q_{k0} + q_{k1}i_1 + \cdots + q_{k,u-1}i_{u-1} + q_{ku}j_u + \cdots + q_{k,k-1}j_{k-1},$$
$$(u \le k \le e);$$

$$p_{k0} + p_{k1}i_1 + \cdots + p_{k,u-1}i_{u-1} + p_{ku}j_u + \cdots + p_{ke}j_e + p_{k,m+1}j_{m+1} + \cdots$$
$$+ p_{k,k-1}j_{k-1}$$
$$\le j_k$$
$$\le q_{k0} + q_{k1}i_1 + \cdots + q_{k,u-1}i_{u-1} + q_{ku}j_u + \cdots + q_{ke}j_e + q_{k,m+1}j_{m+1}$$
$$+ \cdots + q_{k,k-1}j_{k-1},$$
$$(m + 1 \le k \le n);$$

and

$$i_u \leq j_u - 1, \qquad \text{if } 1 \leq u \leq e.$$

(The possible levels are $u = 1, 2,..., e + 1$ for the case $S < T$, and $u = 1, 2,..., e$ for the case $T \leq S$.)

The equations and inequalities can be simplified to a great extent if the loop limits are constant (independent of index variables):

Corollary 2. (Dependence with a given direction vector under constant loop limits and linear subscripts.)

The variables x, y cause a dependence of statement T on statement S with a direction vector $\mathbf{s} = (s_1, s_2,..., s_e)$, iff there is an integer solution to the system of DIM equations

$$(a_{r1}i_1 - b_{r1}j_1) + \cdots + (a_{re}i_e - b_{re}j_e) + a_{r,e+1}i_{e+1} + a_{rm}i_m - b_{r,m+1}j_{m+1} - \cdots - b_{rn}j_n$$

$$= b_{r0} - a_{r0}, \qquad (1 \leq r \leq \text{DIM}),$$

satisfying the conditions:

$$p_k \leq i_k \leq q_k, \qquad (1 \leq k \leq m);$$
$$p_k \leq j_k \leq q_k, \qquad (1 \leq k \leq e \text{ and } m + 1 \leq k \leq n);$$

and
$$i_k - j_k \begin{cases} < 0 & \text{if } s_k = 1 \\ = 0 & \text{if } s_k = 0 \\ > 0 & \text{if } s_k = -1 \end{cases}$$
$$(1 \leq k \leq e).$$

The number of integer variables in the system is $N = e + n - \Omega$, where Ω is the number of zeros in $\mathbf{s}$. (We must have $\mathbf{s} \geq \mathbf{0}$ for the case $S < T$ and $\mathbf{s} > \mathbf{0}$ for the case $T \leq S$.)

Corollary 3. (Dependence at a level under constant loop limits and linear subscripts.)

The variables x, y cause a dependence of statement T on statement S at a level u, iff there is an integer solution to the system of DIM equations

$$(a_{r1} - b_{r1})i_1 + \cdots + (a_{r,u-1} - b_{r,u-1})i_{u-1} + (a_{ru}i_u - b_{ru}j_u) + \cdots$$
$$+ (a_{re}i_e - b_{re}j_e) + a_{r,e+1}i_{e+1} + a_{rm}i_m - b_{r,m+1}j_{m+1} - \cdots - b_{rn}j_n$$

$$= b_{r0} - a_{r0}, \qquad (1 \leq r \leq DIM),$$

in $N = (n + e - u + 1)$ variables, satisfying the conditions:

$$p_k \leq i_k \leq q_k, \qquad (1 \leq k \leq m);$$

$$p_k \leq j_k \leq q_k, \qquad (u \leq k \leq e \text{ and } m + 1 \leq k \leq n);$$

and

$$i_u \leq j_u - 1 \qquad \text{if } 1 \leq u \leq e.$$

(The possible levels are $u = 1, 2,..., e + 1$ for the case $S < T$, and $u = 1, 2,..., e$ for the case $T \leq S$.)

The problem always is to decide whether or not a given set of linear diophantine equations in N variables has an integer solution in a certain region $\Re$ of $\mathbf{R}^N$. If a solution exists, then the specified dependence also exists and the solution itself consists of an iteration pair associated with that dependence. The rest of the book is devoted to this problem. Exact and approximate methods will be derived in Chapter 6, based on computation of bounds of linear functions (Chapter 4) and solution of systems of linear diophantine equations (Chapter 5). We showed in the Introduction (Chapter 1) several examples of these systems of equations and inequalities for actual programs; many more are given in the following pages. Although we do not yet know how to solve such systems, it would be instructive to study the examples at this point just to see how they are formed.

CHAPTER 4

BOUNDS OF LINEAR FUNCTIONS

4.1. INTRODUCTION

We saw in Chapter 3 that to determine if two variables caused a dependence between two statements, with a given direction vector (or at a given level), one must decide if there is an integer solution to a system of linear diophantine equations satisfying a system of linear inequalities (constraints). If the system of equations (without any further constraints) has no integer solution, then there is no dependence. When integer solutions (to the system of equations) are known to exist, there are basically two approaches at that point: find the general solution and see if it can be tailored to fit the constraints, or check certain necessary conditions that must hold if a solution satisfying all constraints is to exist. In Chapter 5, we would lay the groundwork for the first approach by showing how to solve linear diophantine equations. This chapter prepares us for the second approach. Here, the actual expression for the general solution is not needed; we use necessary conditions involving bounds of the linear functions that represent the left hand sides of the equations. A detailed description of this approach is given below:

Let f denote a real valued function on $\mathbf{R}^n$. Suppose f is bounded on a set $\mathfrak{R} \subset \mathbf{R}^n$, and let b denote a lower and B an upper bound in $\mathfrak{R}$. Then we have

$$b \leq f(\mathbf{x}) \leq B, \qquad \text{for each } \mathbf{x} \in \mathbf{R}^n.$$

Hence, for a given real number c, the equation

$$f(\mathbf{x}) = c$$

will have a solution $\mathbf{x} \in \mathfrak{R}$ only if $b \leq c \leq B$. Consider now the converse of this: If $b \leq c \leq B$ holds, does the equation have a solution $\mathbf{x}$ in $\mathfrak{R}$? Under certain restrictions, the converse holds; its precise form is given by the following well-known theorem of advanced calculus:

Theorem 4.1.1. (Intermediate Value Theorem). Let f be a continuous real valued function on $\mathbf{R}^n$. Let b, B denote any two values of f on a connected set $\mathfrak{R} \subset \mathbf{R}^n$, and suppose that $b \leq c \leq B$. Then, the equation

$$f(\mathbf{x}) = c$$

has a solution $\mathbf{x} \in \mathfrak{R}$.

A thorough discussion of the theorem is beyond the scope of this book; see any standard text on advanced calculus. The following example makes one important point: even if c is an integer and f a function that takes integer values at points with integer coordinates, the theorem only guarantees a *real* solution, i.e., a point x in $\mathfrak{R}$ with real coordinates, that satisfies $f(\mathbf{x}) = c$.

Example 4.1.1. The function $f(x, y) = 2x + 3y$ on $\mathbf{R}^2$ and the set

$$\Re = \{(x, y): 0 \le x \le 1, \ 0 \le y \le 1\} \subset \mathbf{R}^2$$

satisfy all requirements of Theorem 4.1.1. We can take $b = 0$ and $B = 5$, since 0 and 5 are values of the function at the points $(0, 0)$ and $(1, 1)$ in $\Re$. For the number 4 between 0 and 5, there must be a solution $(x, y) \in \Re$ to the equation

$$2x + 3y = 4.$$

One such solution is clearly $(1.5, 1)$, and there are many others. Note, however, that there is no *integer* solution: there are four points in $\Re$ with integer coordinates, namely $(0, 0)$, $(0, 1)$, $(1, 0)$, $(1, 1)$, and none of them satisfies the equation.

We now return to the dependence problem. Consider, for example, the simple program

L: **do** $I_1 = 20, 134$
                do $I_2 = I_1 + 1, 200$
S: $A(I_1 + 2*I_2 - 5) = \cdots$
T: $\cdots = \cdots A(3*I_1 + I_2 + 7) \cdots$
                enddo
        enddo

Suppose we want to test if the output variable of statement S and the indicated input variable of statement T cause a flow-dependence of T on S at level 1. We would then look for iterations (i_1, i_2), (j_1, j_2) such that $i_1 < j_1$ and

$$i_1 + 2i_2 - 5 = 3j_1 + j_2 + 7.$$

By Corollary 3 to Theorem 3.2.2, $S \, \delta_1^f T$ holds iff the equation

$$i_1 + 2i_2 - 3j_1 - j_2 = 12 \tag{1}$$

has an integer solution in the subset $\mathfrak{R}$ of $\mathbf{R}^4$ defined by the inequalities:

$$
\begin{aligned}
20 &\le i_1 \le 134 \\
i_1 + 1 &\le i_2 \le 200 \\
20 &\le j_1 \le 134 \\
j_1 + 1 &\le j_2 \le 200 \\
i_1 &\le j_1 - 1.
\end{aligned}
$$

These inequalities can be written as

$$
\begin{aligned}
20 &\le i_1 \le 133 \\
1 + i_1 &\le j_1 \le 134 \\
1 + i_1 &\le i_2 \le 200 \\
1 + j_1 &\le j_2 \le 200.
\end{aligned}
$$

The function under consideration here is $f \colon \mathbf{R}^4 \to \mathbf{R}$ defined by

$$
f(i_1, i_2, j_1, j_2) = i_1 + 2i_2 - 3j_1 - j_2.
$$

Suppose b is a lower bound and B an upper bound of this function in the region $\mathfrak{R}$ described by the above inequalities. If $b \le 12 \le B$ is false, then equation (1) has no real (and hence no integer) solution in $\mathfrak{R}$, and the proposed dependence does not hold. If $b \le 12 \le B$ is true, no conclusion is possible. Even when b, B are values of f on $\mathfrak{R}$, all Theorem 4.1.1 would let us conclude is that there is a *real* solution to (1) in $\mathfrak{R}$. To be on the safe side, we would *assume* in this case that an integer solution also exists. (If dependence is assumed where there is none, it may lead to some loss in parallelism, but never to an invalid program transformation based on dependence analysis.)

The tighter are the bounds, the better is the chance that the above method would be decisive. Ideally, the bounds should be values of the function in the region, i.e., the lower bound should be the minimum and the upper bound the maximum value of f in $\mathfrak{R}$ (Lemma 4.1.2(1) below).

Although the dependence problem deals with integer solutions, there is no advantage in working with integers for this particular method. We consider a real valued linear function f on $\mathbf{R}^n$, defined by

$$f(\mathbf{x}) = a_1 x_1 + a_2 x_2 + \cdots + a_n x_n$$

where $\mathbf{x} = (x_1, x_2,..., x_n)$ and $a_1, a_2,..., a_n$ are real constants. The region $\Re \subset \mathbf{R}^n$ is either a *rectangle*

$$\{\mathbf{x} \in \mathbf{R}^n: p_1 \leq x_1 \leq q_1, \ p_2 \leq x_2 \leq q_2,..., \ p_n \leq x_n \leq q_n\}$$

where p_k, q_k are real constants ($1 \leq k \leq n$), or, more generally, a *trapezoid* given by a set of inequalities:

$$p_{10} \leq x_1 \leq q_{10}$$
$$p_{20} + p_{21}x_1 \leq x_2 \leq q_{20} + q_{21}x_1$$
$$\vdots$$
$$p_{n0} + p_{n1}x_1 + \cdots + p_{n,n-1}x_{n-1} \leq x_n \leq q_{n0} + q_{n1}x_1 + \cdots + q_{n,n-1}x_{n-1},$$

where the coefficients p_{kr} and q_{kr} are real constants, $1 \leq k \leq n$, $0 \leq r \leq k - 1$. A simple technique for computation of tight lower and upper bounds of f in $\Re$ is developed in this chapter. These bounds have closed expressions and are the extreme values of f, always when $\Re$ is a rectangle, and frequently when $\Re$ is a trapezoid.

We start Section 4.2 with the concept of positive and negative parts of a number, which is very useful in producing expressions that combine different cases based on signs of parameters. Bounds of linear functions in rectangular regions are then studied in the same section. Those results are extended to trapezoids in $\mathbf{R}^n$ in Section 4.3. The key results are Lemma 4.2.2, Theorem 4.2.3, and Algorithm 4.3.1 giving the bounds in an interval, an n-dimensional rectangle, and a general n-dimensional trapezoid, respectively. We will give a couple of examples to demonstrate the dependence testing method outlined above; the method itself will be studied in detail in Chapter 6.

We assume the reader is familiar with the elementary facts about bounds and extreme values of arbitrary real-valued functions (discussed in calculus texts). Lemma 4.1.2 is a collection of results we will need.

Lemma 4.1.2. Let f be a real-valued function on an arbitrary set X, and let Y, Z denote two subsets of X. Then the following hold:

1. If a lower (upper) bound of f in X equals the value $f(x)$ at some point $x \in X$, then $f(x)$ is the minimum (maximum) value of f in X.

2. If $Y \subset Z$, a lower (upper) bound of f in Z is also a lower (upper) bound in Y.

3. If b is a lower bound of f in Y and b´ a lower bound in Z, then $\min\{b, b´\}$ is a lower bound in $Y \cup Z$ and $\max\{b, b´\}$ a lower bound in $Y \cap Z$.

4. If B is an upper bound of f in Y and B´ an upper bound in Z, then $\max\{B, B´\}$ is an upper bound in $Y \cup Z$ and $\min\{B, B´\}$ an upper bound in $Y \cap Z$.

4.2. BOUNDS IN RECTANGLES

The positive part a^+ and the negative part a^- of a real number a are defined by
$$a^+ = \max\{a, 0\}$$
and
$$a^- = \max\{-a, 0\}.$$

In other words, $a^+ = a$, $a^- = 0$ for $a \geq 0$, and $a^+ = 0$, $a^- = -a$ for $a \leq 0$. Thus, $4^+ = 4$, $4^- = 0$, $(-4)^+ = 0$, $(-4)^- = 4$. The basic properties of positive and negative parts are listed below. They will be used rather heavily in this book, usually without any explicit reference.

Lemma 4.2.1. For any real number a, the following hold:

1. $a^+ \geq 0$, $a^- \geq 0$.

2. $a = a^+ - a^-$, $\quad |a| = a^+ + a^-$.

3. $(-a)^+ = a^-$, $\quad (-a)^- = a^+$.

4. $(a^+)^+ = a^+$, $\qquad (a^+)^- = 0$,
   $(a^-)^+ = a^-$, $\qquad (a^-)^- = 0$.

5. $-a^- \leq a \leq a^+$.

PROOF. The proof is trivial and is left to the reader. Separate consideration of the two cases $a \geq 0$ and $a < 0$, although not always necessary, will usually help. ♦

Lemma 4.2.2 uses positive and negative parts to conveniently express the extreme values of a simple function. More advanced results that come later are based on this.

Lemma 4.2.2. If $p \leq x \leq q$, then

$$a^+p - a^-q \leq ax \leq a^+q - a^-p.$$

Indeed, if $p \leq q$ then $(a^+p - a^-q)$ is the minimum and $(a^+q - a^-p)$ the maximum value of the function $f(x) = ax$ in the closed interval $[p, q]$.

PROOF. Since $a^+ \geq 0$ and $-a^- \geq 0$, we derive from $p \leq x \leq q$ that

$$a^+p \leq a^+x \leq a^+q$$
and
$$-a^-q \leq -a^-x \leq -a^-p.$$

Add these two sets of inequalities to get

$$a^+p - a^-q \leq (a^+ - a^-)x \leq a^+q - a^-p.$$

Since $a = a^+ - a^-$, we have proved the first part of the lemma.

For the second part, note that $(a^+p - a^-q)$ is a lower bound and $(a^+q - a^-p)$ an upper bound for $f(x) = ax$ in $[p, q]$. But, these bounds are actually values of the function at the end points $x = p, q$. For example, when $a \geq 0$ we have

$$a^+p - a^-q = ap = f(p)$$
and
$$a^+q - a^-p = aq = f(q).$$

Hence, the lower bound $(a^+p - a^-q)$ is the minimum and the upper bound $(a^+q - a^-p)$ the maximum value of f in $[p, q]$, (Lemma 4.1.2(1)). ◆

Example 4.2.1. The function $g(x) = 2x$ is monotonically increasing; its minimum value in the interval $[-1, 2]$ is attained at $x = -1$ and the maximum value at $x = 2$. The function $h(x) = -2x$ is monotonically decreasing; its minimum value in the same interval is attained at $x = 2$, and the maximum value at $x = -1$. Both cases are handled by the lemma which gives $(-a^+ - 2a^-)$ as the minimum and $(2a^+ + a^-)$ as the maximum value of the function $f(x) = ax$ in $[-1, 2]$.

We next generalize Lemma 4.2.2 to the case of a linear function in n variables.

Theorem 4.2.3. If
$$p_k \leq x_k \leq q_k, \qquad\qquad (1 \leq k \leq n),$$
then
$$\sum_{k=1}^{n} (a_k^+ p_k - a_k^- q_k) \leq \sum_{k=1}^{n} a_k x_k \leq \sum_{k=1}^{n} (a_k^+ q_k - a_k^- p_k).$$

More precisely, if the rectangle $\Re \subset \mathbf{R}^n$, defined by

$$\Re = \{(x_1, x_2,..., x_n):\ p_1 \leq x_1 \leq q_1,\ p_2 \leq x_2 \leq q_2,...,\ p_n \leq x_n \leq q_n\},$$

is nonempty, then the minimum and maximum values of the function $f(x) = \Sigma\, a_k x_k$ in $\Re$ are respectively $\Sigma(a_k^+ p_k - a_k^- q_k)$ and $\Sigma(a_k^+ q_k - a_k^- p_k)$.

PROOF. Since $p_k \le x_k \le q_k$, it follows from Lemma 4.2.2 that

$$a_k^+ p_k - a_k^- q_k \;\le\; a_k x_k \;\le\; a_k^+ q_k - a_k^- p_k, \qquad (1 \le k \le n).$$

Summing over k, we get the first part.

It is clear that $\Sigma(a_k^+ p_k - a_k^- q_k)$ is a lower and $\Sigma(a_k^+ q_k - a_k^- p_k)$ an upper bound for f in $\Re$. The function actually attains these bounds at some points in the set

$$\{(x_1, x_2,..., x_n):\ x_1 = p_1 \text{ or } q_1,\ x_2 = p_2 \text{ or } q_2,...,\ x_n = p_n \text{ or } q_n\}.$$

(This is the set of vertices of the rectangle.) For example, we have

$$\Sigma(a_k^+ p_k - a_k^- q_k) = f(x_1, x_2,..., x_n),$$

where $x_k = p_k$ if $a_k \ge 0$ and $x_k = q_k$ if $p_k < 0$, $(1 \le k \le n)$. Hence, the lower bound is the minimum and the upper bound the maximum value of f in $\Re$ (Lemma 4.1.2(1)). ◆

Example 4.2.2. To find the bounds of the function

$$f(x_1, x_2, x_3) = 2x_1 - 3x_2 + x_3$$

in the rectangle

$$\Re = \{(x_1, x_2, x_3) \in \mathbf{R}^3:\ -1 \le x_1 \le 2,\ 0 \le x_2 \le 1,\ 2 \le x_3 \le 4\},$$

note that here
$$p_1 = -1,\ q_1 = 2,\ p_2 = 0,\ q_2 = 1,\ p_3 = 2,\ q_3 = 4,$$
$$a_1 = 2,\ a_2 = -3,\ \text{and } a_3 = 1.$$

Using the formulas in the theorem, we have for $(x_1, x_2, x_3) \in \Re$,

$$\sum_{k=1}^{3} (a_k^+ p_k - a_k^- q_k) \le \sum_{k=1}^{3} a_k x_k \le \sum_{k=1}^{3} (a_k^+ q_k - a_k^- p_k),$$

or $(2^+(-1) - 2^-\cdot 2) + ((-3)^+\cdot 0 - (-3)^-\cdot 1) + (1^+\cdot 2 - 1^-\cdot 4)$

$\le \ 2x_1 - 3x_2 + x_3$

$\le \ (2^+\cdot 2 - 2^-(-1)) + ((-3)^+\cdot 1 - (-3)^-\cdot 0) + (1^+\cdot 4 - 1^-\cdot 2),$

or
$$-3 \le 2x_1 - 3x_2 + x_3 \le 8.$$

Also, $-3 = f(-1, 1, 2)$ is the minimum and $8 = f(2, 0, 4)$ the maximum value of f in $\Re$.

To get a better understanding of why these formulas work, we now compute the bounds directly. Observe that

$$-1 \le x_1 \le 2 \quad \text{implies} \quad -2 \le 2x_1 \le 4,$$
$$0 \le x_2 \le 1 \quad \text{implies} \quad -3 \le -3x_2 \le 0,$$

and we have
$$2 \le x_3 \le 4.$$

Adding the three final sets of inequalities, we get

$$-3 \le 2x_1 - 3x_2 + x_3 \le 8.$$

The formulas for bounds take care of all possible combinations of signs of the coefficients in the function (which are 2, -3, 1 in this example), so that the direction of an inequality is automatically reversed if it is multiplied by a negative number (as in the case of $-3x_2$ above).

Example 4.2.3. Consider the double loop

$$\textbf{do } I_1 = 1, 10$$
$$\textbf{do } I_2 = 1, 10$$

S: $A(I_1 - 2I_2 - 11) = \cdots$

T: $A(-I_1 + I_2 + 8) = \cdots$

$$\textbf{enddo}$$
$$\textbf{enddo}$$

Statement T would be output dependent on statement S at level 3, if there is an iteration (i_1, i_2) such that the elements $A(i_1 - 2i_2 - 11)$ and $A(-i_1 + i_2 + 8)$ represent the same memory loacation. In other words, the dependence $S \, \delta_3^o \, T$ holds iff there is an integer solution to the equation

$$2i_1 - 3i_2 = 19 \tag{1}$$

subject to the constraints

$$1 \leq i_1 \leq 10 \quad \text{and} \quad 1 \leq i_2 \leq 10. \tag{2}$$

Using the formulas for bounds in Theorem 4.2.3, we get

$$-28 \leq 2i_1 - 3i_2 \leq 17$$

for each point (i_1, i_2) that satisfies (2). Since 19 does not lie between -28 and 17, there is no solution (real or integer) to (1) that also satisfies (2). Hence, the dependence $S \, \delta_3^o \, T$ does not hold.

4.3. BOUNDS IN TRAPEZOIDS

Here we extend the method of the last section to compute bounds of a linear function in a trapezoid. Closed-form expressions for bounds, although still possible, are generally too complicated to write down; we give an algorithm instead. There is, however, one special case which will be very useful for dependence tests in Chapter 6. We state below the results of this case in the form of a lemma. As an additional benefit, the proof of this lemma will illustrate the steps of the algorithm that would follow.

Lemma 4.3.1. If $0 \leq x \leq q$ and $0 \leq y \leq x$, then

$$-(a - b^-)^- q \; \leq \; ax + by \; \leq \; (a + b^+)^+ q.$$

Indeed, these bounds are the extreme values of the function $f(x, y) = ax + by$ in the triangle

$$\Re = \{(x, y) \in \mathbf{R}^2 \colon 0 \leq x \leq q \text{ and } 0 \leq y \leq x\}.$$

PROOF. By Lemma 4.2.2, we get

$$-b^- x \; \leq \; by \; \leq \; b^+ x,$$

so that

$$(a - b^-)x \; \leq \; ax + by \; \leq \; (a + b^+)x.$$

Another application of the same lemma, this time using the inequality $0 \leq x \leq q$, yields the expressions for the bounds of $ax + by$.

The second part follows as in the proofs of Lemma 4.2.2 and Theorem 4.2.3: the bounds are always values of the function f on $\Re$. We leave it to the reader to show that each of the expressions equals the value at one of the points $\{(1, 0), (q, 0), (q, q - 1)\}$ under any possible assignment of signs to a, b, $a + b$, and $a - b$. ◆

The following algorithm uses this process of elimination repeatedly to find the bounds of a linear function in a general trapezoid. The bounds, however, may no longer be the extreme values of the function; we will return to this point in Remark 4.3.1.

Algorithm 4.3.1. Given a linear function

$$f(\mathbf{x}) = a_1 x_1 + a_2 x_2 + \cdots + a_n x_n$$

and a nonempty trapezoidal region $\mathfrak{R} \subset \mathbf{R}^n$, defined by a set of inequalities of the form

$$p_{10} \le x_1 \le q_{10}$$
$$p_{20} + p_{21}x_1 \le x_2 \le q_{20} + q_{21}x_1$$
$$\vdots$$
$$p_{n0} + p_{n1}x_1 + \cdots + p_{n,n-1}x_{n-1} \le x_n \le q_{n0} + q_{n1}x_1 + \cdots + q_{n,n-1}x_{n-1},$$

where the coefficients a_k, p_{kr} and q_{kr} are real constants ($1 \le k \le n$, $0 \le r \le k - 1$), this algorithm finds a lower bound $b_{low} \equiv b_{low}(f, \mathfrak{R})$ and an upper bound $b_{up} \equiv b_{up}(f, \mathfrak{R})$ for f in $\mathfrak{R}$.

1. [Initialize.] Set $b_{low} \leftarrow 0, b_{up} \leftarrow 0$;
$$k \leftarrow n;$$

$$(d_1, d_2,..., d_k) \leftarrow (a_1, a_2,..., a_k),$$
$$(e_1, e_2,..., e_k) \leftarrow (a_1, a_2,..., a_k).$$

2. [Eliminate x_k.] Set $b_{low} \leftarrow b_{low} + d_k^+ p_{k0} - d_k^- q_{k0}$

$$b_{up} \leftarrow b_{up} + e_k^+ q_{k0} - e_k^- p_{k0}.$$

If $k > 1$, then set
$$(d_1, d_2,..., d_{k-1}) \leftarrow (d_1 + d_k^+ p_{k1} - d_k^- q_{k1}, d_2 + d_k^+ p_{k2} - d_k^- q_{k2},...,$$

$$d_{k-1} + d_k^+ p_{k,k-1} - d_k^- q_{k,k-1}),$$

$$(e_1, e_2,..., e_{k-1}) \leftarrow (e_1 + e_k^+ q_{k1} - e_k^- p_{k1}, e_2 + e_k^+ q_{k2} - e_k^- p_{k2},...,$$

$$e_{k-1} + e_k^+ q_{k,k-1} - e_k^- p_{k,k-1}),$$

$$k \leftarrow k - 1;$$

and go to **2**. Otherwise, halt.

PROOF. Let $(x_1, x_2,..., x_n)$ denote any point in $\Re$. For $1 \le k \le n$, we have

$$p_{k0} + p_{k1}x_1 + \cdots + p_{k,k-1}x_{k-1} \le x_k \le q_{k0} + q_{k1}x_1 + \cdots + q_{k,k-1}x_{k-1}.$$

The algorithm starts with the expression $(a_1x_1 + a_2x_2 + ... + a_nx_n)$ and using the above relations, eliminates one variable at a time in the reverse order $x_n, x_{n-1},..., x_1$. Since

$$p_{n0} + p_{n1}x_1 + \cdots + p_{n,n-1}x_{n-1} \le x_n \le q_{n0} + q_{n1}x_1 + \cdots + q_{n,n-1}x_{n-1},$$

it follows from Lemma 4.2.2 that

$$(a_n^+ p_{n0} - a_n^- q_{n0}) + (a_1 + a_n^+ p_{n1} - a_n^- q_{n1})x_1 - (a_2 + a_n^+ p_{n2} - a_n^- q_{n2})x_2$$

$$+ \cdots + (a_{n-1} + a_n^+ p_{n,n-1} - a_n^- q_{n,n-1})x_{n-1}$$

$$\le a_1x_1 + a_2x_2 + \cdots + a_nx_n$$

$$\le (a_n^+ q_{n0} - a_n^- p_{n0}) + (a_1 + a_n^+ q_{n1} - a_n^- p_{n1})x_1 - (a_2 + a_n^+ q_{n2} - a_n^- p_{n2})x_2$$

$$+ \cdots + (a_{n-1} + a_n^+ q_{n,n-1} - a_n^- p_{n,n-1})x_{n-1}$$

Initially, we have
$$(b_{low}, d_1, d_2,..., d_n) = (0, a_1, a_2,..., a_n)$$
and
$$(b_{up}, e_1, e_2,..., e_n) = (0, a_1, a_2,..., a_n).$$

After step 2 has been executed for the first time, the new values of $(b_{low}, d_1, d_2,..., d_{n-1})$ and $(b_{up}, e_1, e_2,..., e_{n-1})$ satisfy

$$b_{low} + d_1x_1 + d_2x_2 + \cdots + d_{n-1}x_{n-1}$$
$$\le a_1x_1 + a_2x_2 + \cdots + a_nx_n$$
$$\le b_{up} + e_1x_1 + e_2x_2 + \cdots + e_{n-1}x_{n-1}.$$

Next, we use the inequalities in (1) for x_{n-1}, and invoking Lemma 4.2.2 twice, get two expressions in $x_1, x_2,..., x_{n-2}$: one less than $(b_{low} + d_1x_1 + d_2x_2 + \cdots + d_{n-1}x_{n-1})$ and the other greater than $(b_{up} + e_1x_1 + e_2x_2 + \cdots + e_{n-1}x_{n-1})$. The coefficients in these expressions constitute the values assigned to $(b_{low}, d_1, d_2,..., d_{n-2})$, $(b_{up}, e_1, e_2,..., e_{n-2})$ for the third time. After t executions of step 2, the current values of $(b_{low}, d_1, d_2,..., d_{n-t})$, $(b_{up}, e_1, e_2,..., e_{n-t})$ satisfy

$$b_{low} + d_1x_1 + d_2x_2 + \cdots + d_{n-k}x_{n-t}$$
$$\leq a_1x_1 + a_2x_2 + \cdots + a_nx_n$$
$$\leq b_{up} + e_1x_1 + e_2x_2 + \cdots + e_{n-k}x_{n-t}.$$

After n executions, only the constant terms remain:

$$b_{low} \leq a_1x_1 + a_2x_2 + \cdots + a_nx_n \leq b_{up}.$$

Thus, the final values of b_{low} and b_{up} give a lower and an upper bound, respectively, for the function f in the region $\Re$. ♦

By this algorithm and Lemma 4.1.2, we can compute a set of bounds in any region that can be expressed as a finite combination of trapezoids, (i.e., can be constructed from a finite number of trapezoids using a finite number of operations of union and intersection).

Example 4.3.1. Consider $f(x,y) = -x + 2y$ in the region $\Re$ defined by

$$1 \leq x \leq 2$$
$$7 - 3x \leq y \leq 4 + x.$$

From the inequalities on y, we have

$$14 - 6x \leq 2y \leq 8 + 2x,$$
so that
$$14 - 7x \leq -x + 2y \leq 8 + x.$$

Then $1 \leq x \leq 2$ implies $-14 \leq -7x \leq -7$. It follows that

$$0 \leq -x + 2y \leq 10.$$

We show below how these bounds can be derived by Algorithm 4.3.1. Remember that here $n = 2$, $a_1 = -1$, $a_2 = 2$, $p_{10} = 1$, $q_{10} = 2$, $p_{20} = 7$, $p_{21} = -3$, $q_{20} = 4$, and $q_{21} = 1$.

[Initialize.] Set $\qquad b_{low} \leftarrow 0, b_{up} \leftarrow 0;$
$\qquad\qquad\qquad\qquad (d_1, d_2) \leftarrow (-1, 2),$
$\qquad\qquad\qquad\qquad (e_1, e_2) \leftarrow (-1, 2).$

[Eliminate x_2.] Set

$$b_{low} \leftarrow b_{low} + d_2^+ p_{20} - d_2^- q_{20} = 14$$

$$b_{up} \leftarrow b_{up} + e_2^+ q_{20} - e_2^- p_{20} = 8.$$

$$d_1 \leftarrow d_1 + d_2^+ p_{21} - d_2^- q_{21} = -7$$

$$e_1 \leftarrow e_1 + e_2^+ q_{21} - e_2^- p_{21} = 1$$

[Eliminate x_1.] Set

$$b_{low} \leftarrow b_{low} + d_1^+ p_{10} - d_1^- q_{10} = 0$$

$$b_{up} \leftarrow b_{up} + e_1^+ q_{10} - e_1^- p_{10} = 10.$$

Halt.

We see that $f(2, 1) = 0$ and $f(2, 6) = 10$, where $(2, 1)$ and $(2, 6)$ are points in the region. This implies (Lemma 4.1.2(1)) that 0 is the minimum and 10 the maximum value of the function f in $\Re$.

Example 4.3.2. Consider $f(x,y) = 3x + y$ in the region $\Re$ defined by

$$2 \leq x \leq 4$$
$$x \leq y \leq 6 - x.$$

Using the inequalities on y, we get $4x \le 3x + y \le 6 + 2x$. Then the inequalities on x yield $8 \le 3x + y \le 14$. Since the point $(2, 2)$ is in $\Re$ and $f(2, 2) = 8$, it follows that 8 is the minimum value of f in $\Re$. However, 14 is not the maximum value. Note that we have $x \le y \le 6 - x$, so that $2x \le 6$, or $x \le 3$. Hence,

$$3x + y \le 3x + 6 - x = 2x + 6 \le 12.$$

The reader should carry out the steps of the algorithm to derive these bounds.

Example 4.3.3. Suppose we want to find a set of bounds for the function $f(x,y,z) = 2x - y - 4z$ in the region $\Re \subset \mathbf{R}^3$, defined by

$$1 \le x \le 5$$
$$3 - 2x \le y \le 1 + 3x$$
$$1 + x - y \le z \le 2 - x + 2y.$$

This is how Algorithm 4.3.1 would work: Note first that

$$-4(2 - x + 2y) \le -4z \le -4(1 + x - y).$$

Using this, we get after some simplification,

$$-8 + 6x - 9y \le 2x - y - 4z \le -4 - 2x + 3y.$$

Now, $-9(1 + 3x) \le -9y$ and $3y \le 3(1 + 3x)$, so that

$$-17 - 21x \le 2x - y - 4z \le -1 + 7x.$$

Finally, x is eliminated to yield the bounds

$$-122 \le 2x - y - 4z \le 34.$$

These bounds also happen to be the extreme values of f in $\Re$, since $-122 = f(5, 16, 29)$, $34 = f(5, 16, -10)$ and the points $(5, 16, 29)$, $(5, 16, -10)$ lie in $\Re$, (Lemma 4.1.2(1)).

Example 4.3.4. Consider the program

$$\textbf{do } I_1 = 1, 100$$
$$\quad \textbf{do } I_2 = I_1, 50$$

S: $\qquad A(I_1 - I_2 + 11) = \cdots$

T: $\qquad\qquad \cdots = \cdots A(-2*I_1 + I_2 + 23) \cdots$

$$\quad \textbf{enddo}$$
$$\textbf{enddo}$$

Suppose we want to test if the output variable $A(I_1 - I_2 + 11)$ of statement S and the input variable $A(-2*I_1 + I_2 + 23)$ of statement T cause T to be flow-dependent on S at level 1. In order for this dependence to hold, there must exist iterations (i_1, i_2) and (j_1, j_2) such that $(i_1, i_2) <_1 (j_1, j_2)$, and the variables $A(i_1 - i_2 + 11)$, $A(-2j_1 + j_2 + 23)$ represent the same memory location. Thus, we are looking for an integer solution to the equation

$$i_1 - i_2 + 11 = -2j_1 + j_2 + 23,$$

subject to the conditions

$$1 \le i_1 \le 100$$
$$i_1 \le i_2 \le 50$$
$$1 \le j_1 \le 100$$
$$j_1 \le j_2 \le 50$$

and

$$i_1 < j_1.$$

The equation and the conditions are rewritten as follows:

$$i_1 - i_2 + 2j_1 - j_2 = 12, \qquad\qquad (1)$$

and

$$1 \le i_1 \le 99$$
$$i_1 \le i_2 \le 50 \qquad\qquad (2)$$
$$1 + i_1 \le j_1 \le 100$$
$$j_1 \le j_2 \le 50.$$

Here the function is $f:\mathbf{R}^4 \rightarrow \mathbf{R}$ defined by

$$f(i_1, i_2, j_1, j_2) = i_1 - i_2 + 2j_1 - j_2$$

which is the left hand side of (1), and the region is the trapezoid $\mathfrak{R} \subset \mathbf{R}^4$ defined by the inequalities in (2). To find the bounds of f in $\mathfrak{R}$ we apply Algorithm 4.3.1.

First eliminate j_2:

$$-50 + i_1 - i_2 + 2j_1 \le i_1 - i_2 + 2j_1 - j_2 \le i_1 - i_2 + j_1,$$

then j_1:

$$-48 + 3i_1 - i_2 \le i_1 - i_2 + 2j_1 - j_2 \le 100 + i_1 - i_2,$$

next i_2:

$$-98 + 3i_1 \le i_1 - i_2 + 2j_1 - j_2 \le 100,$$

and finally i_1:

$$-95 \le i_1 - i_2 + 2j_1 - j_2 \le 100.$$

Thus, -95 is a lower and 100 an upper bound of the function f in the region $\mathfrak{R}$. Since 12, the right hand side of (1), lies between -95 and 100, the dependence testing method sketched in Section 4.1 fails. As mentioned there, we assume in this case that the indicated dependence exists. In fact, there is dependence—iterations (i_1, i_2) = (1, 8) and (j_1, j_2) = (20, 21) satisfy all the requirements. (There are other iteration pairs as well.)

Notation. The function f can be specified by an n-vector $(a_1, a_2, ..., a_n)$, and the region $\mathfrak{R}$ by two $n \times n$ lower triangular matrices

$$P = \begin{bmatrix} p_{10} & 0 & 0 & \cdots & 0 \\ p_{20} & p_{21} & 0 & \cdots & 0 \\ \vdots & \vdots & \vdots & \cdots & \vdots \\ p_{n0} & p_{n1} & \cdot & \cdots & p_{n,n-1} \end{bmatrix}$$

and

$$Q = \begin{bmatrix} q_{10} & 0 & 0 & \cdots & 0 \\ q_{20} & q_{21} & 0 & \cdots & 0 \\ \vdots & \vdots & \vdots & \cdots & \vdots \\ q_{n0} & q_{n1} & \cdot & \cdots & q_{n,n-1} \end{bmatrix}.$$

Each of the b-functions b_{low} and b_{up} is a function of $n(n + 2)$ parameters (n parameters for f, and $n(n + 1)/2$ parameters for each matrix). Lemma 4.2.2, Theorem 4.2.3, and Lemma 4.3.1 give closed-form expressions for $b_{low}(f, \Re)$ and $b_{up}(f, \Re)$ in the cases where $\Re$ is an interval, an n-dimensional rectangle, and a special 2-dimensional triangle, respectively.

We now make some general observations on the relationship between the bounds b_{low}, b_{up} and the extreme values of a function in a given region.

Remark 4.3.1. Consider the region $\Re$ of Algorithm 4.3.1. Let X denote the set of 2^n points $(x_1, x_2,..., x_n)$ in $\mathbf{R}^n$ such that

$x_1 = p_{10}$ or q_{10}

$x_2 = (p_{20} + p_{21}x_1)$ or $(q_{20} + q_{21}x_1)$

$\vdots$

$x_n = (p_{n0} + p_{n1}x_1 + \cdots + p_{n,n-1}x_{n-1})$ or $(q_{n0} + q_{n1}x_1 + \cdots + q_{n,n-1}x_{n-1})$.

There are two points **y**, **z** in this set such that the numbers b_{low} and b_{up} computed by Algorithm 4.3.1 are values of the function $f(x_1, x_2,..., x_n) = \Sigma\ a_k x_k$ at these points, i.e.,

$$b_{low}(f, \Re) = f(\mathbf{y}) \quad \text{and} \quad b_{up}(f, \Re) = f(\mathbf{z}).$$

If $\Re$ is nonempty, b_{low} is a lower bound and b_{up} an upper bound of f in $\Re$. A sufficient condition for b_{low} to be the minimum value of f in $\Re$ is that $\mathbf{y} \in \Re$, and a sufficient condition for b_{up} to be the maximum value of f in $\Re$ is that $\mathbf{z} \in \Re$, (Lemma 4.1.2(1)). Both of these happen when $X \subset \Re$. It was easy to see that $X \subset \Re$ in case of a nonempty n-dimensional rectangle or the simple 2-dimensional traingle of Lemma 4.3.1. For a general n-dimensional trapezoid $\Re$, it is much harder to decide whether $\Re$ is empty, or whether $X \subset \Re$. Algorithm 4.3.1 is simple-minded in the sense that it does not consider all possible pairs of inequalities from each of which a variable may be eliminated. In the general case, to decide if the region is nonempty, or to find the precise extreme values of a function in the region, one has to resort to linear programming or some systematic method of variable elimination. Complicated regions seldom arise in dependence problems; Theorem 4.2.3 and Lemma 4.3.1 are usually adequate.

If it turns out that $b_{low}(f, \Re) > b_{up}(f, \Re)$ for some function f in some region $\Re$, then that would indicate an inconsistency in the system of inequalities defining $\Re$, so that $\Re$ would be empty in that case. For a 2-dimensional trapezoid, there are simple conditions for nonemptiness of $\Re$ and X being contained in $\Re$:

The trapezoid $\Re = \{(x, y): p \leq x \leq q, \ p_0 + p_1 x \leq y \leq q_0 + q_1 x\}$ is nonempty, iff

$$p \leq q$$

and $\qquad p_0 - q_0 \leq (q_1 - p_1)^+ q - (q_1 - p_1)^- p.$

We have $X \subset \Re$ if

$$p \leq q$$

and $\qquad p_0 - q_0 \leq (q_1 - p_1)^+ p - (q_1 - p_1)^- q.$

Remark 4.3.2. Suppose we want to find the bounds of the function $f(x, y) = x + y$ in the region

$$\{(x, y) \in \mathbf{R}^2: \ 0 \leq x \leq 5, \ 1 - x \leq y \leq x\}.$$

Eliminating y using $1 - x \leq y \leq x$, we get $1 \leq x + y \leq 2x$. Next, we eliminate x and find that $1 \leq x + y \leq 10$. Note that we could first find the bounds of y as a function of x, namely −4 and 5, and use those to get $-4 \leq x + y \leq 10$. That method yields a lower bound of −4 which is clearly worse than the lower bound of 1. This happens, because in the second approach, we have expanded our region to the square $\{(x, y) \in \mathbf{R}^2: \ 0 \leq x \leq 5, \ -4 \leq y \leq 5\}$, increasing thereby the possibility that the bounds would be less tight.

CHAPTER 5

LINEAR DIOPHANTINE EQUATIONS

5.1. INTRODUCTION

A linear diophantine equation has the form

$$a_1x_1 + a_2x_2 + \cdots + a_nx_n = c$$

where a_1, a_2,..., a_n, c are integer constants and x_1, x_2,..., x_n are integer variables. As we saw in Chapter 3, these equations play a very important role in the linear dependence problem. In this chapter we study how to decide if there is a solution to a given linear diophantine equation or a system of such equations, when no further constraints are present. In either case, if a solution exists, a formula for the general solution is also obtained. A brief coverage of the greatest common divisor is given in Section 5.2, and the well-known method for solution of a single equation in two variables is described in Section 5.3. The next two sections deal with single equations in many variables and systems of equations. It is assumed that the reader is familiar with elementary properties of the greatest common divisor and basic linear algebra. For details on the gcd and Euclid's algorithm, see the excellent treatment in [Knuth 1980, Section 4.5.2]. The matrix methods used in sections 5.4, 5.5 are taken from [Kertzner 1981]; we have changed his notation and given detailed proofs and algorithms. A discussion of some of the matrix theory concepts involved there is to be found in the appendix added to this chapter. See also a number theory book, e.g., [Kirch 1974].

We will insert some dependence examples at suitable locations to indicate how diophantine equations are to be used in dependence tests which are formally developed in Chapter 6. Even for integers a, b, we use a/b to denote the real quotient. The statement "a divides b" means "a divides b *evenly*," i.e., b mod a is zero and a/b is an integer. Also, unless otherwise stated, by a solution to a system of diophantine equations, we always mean an *integer* solution.

5.2. GREATEST COMMON DIVISORS

If a, b are integers, not both zero, then their *greatest common divisor*, $\gcd(a, b)$, is the largest positive integer that (evenly) divides both a and b. We define $\gcd(0, 0) = 0$. The basic properties of the gcd are stated without proof in Lemma 5.2.1, and then a modern version of Euclid's algorithm is given.

Lemma 5.2.1. Let a, b denote integers. Then

1. $\gcd(a, b) \geq 0$, and $\gcd(a, b) = 0$ iff $a = b = 0$,
2. $\gcd(a, b) = \gcd(|a|, |b|)$,

3. $\gcd(a, 0) = |a|$,
4. $\gcd(a, 1) = 1$,
5. $\gcd(b, a) = \gcd(a, b)$,
6. $\gcd(-a, b) = \gcd(a, b)$,
7. $\gcd(qa, qb) = |q| \cdot \gcd(a, b)$ for any integer q,
8. $\gcd(a - qb, b) = \gcd(a, b)$ for any integer q,
9. If $d = \gcd(a, b) > 0$, then the integers a/d and b/d are relatively prime (i.e., have no common factors other than 1).

Algorithm 5.2.1. (Euclid's Algorithm). Given two integers a, b, this algorithm finds $d \equiv \gcd(a, b)$.

1. Set $u \leftarrow |a|$ and $v \leftarrow |b|$.

2. If $v = 0$, then set $d \leftarrow u$ and terminate the algorithm.

3. Set $r \leftarrow u \bmod v$, $u \leftarrow v$, and $v \leftarrow r$. Go to 2.   ♦

There is also an efficient binary gcd algorithm discovered by J. Stein, [Knuth 1980, Section 4.5.2, Algorithm B].

If $a_1, a_2,..., a_n$ are integers, not all zero, their *greatest common divisor*, $\gcd(a_1, a_2,..., a_n)$, is the largest positive integer that (evenly) divides each a_i. When $a_1 = a_2 = \cdots = a_n = 0$, we define the gcd to be 0. The following represents, for the most part, a generalized version of Lemma 5.2.1:

Lemma 5.2.2. Let $a_1, a_2,..., a_n$ denote integers. Then

1. $\gcd(a_1, a_2,..., a_n) \geq 0$, and
   $\gcd(a_1, a_2,..., a_n) = 0$ iff $a_1 = a_2 = \cdots = a_n = 0$,
2. $\gcd(a_1, a_2,..., a_n) = \gcd(|a_1|, |a_2|,..., |a_n|)$,
3. $\gcd(a_1, a_2,..., a_n, 0) = \gcd(a_1, a_2,..., a_n)$,

4. $\gcd(a_1, a_2,..., a_n, 1) = 1$,
5. $\gcd(b_1, b_2,..., b_n) = \gcd(a_1, a_2,..., a_n)$
     where $b_1, b_2,..., b_n$ is any permutation of $a_1, a_2,..., a_n$,
6. $\gcd(qa_1, qa_2,..., qa_n) = |q| \cdot \gcd(a_1, a_2,..., a_n)$
     for any integer q,
7. $\gcd(a_1, a_2,..., a_n) = \gcd(a_1, \gcd(a_2, a_3,..., a_n))$.

Using some of these properties and Algorithm 5.2.1, we can compute the gcd of any finite set of numbers.

Algorithm 5.2.2. Given a positive integer n and a set of n integers $a_1, a_2,..., a_n$, this algorithm finds $d \equiv \gcd(a_1, a_2,..., a_n)$.

1. Set $d \leftarrow a_n$, $i \leftarrow n - 1$.

2. If $d = 1$ or $i = 0$, then $d = \gcd(a_1, a_2,..., a_n)$ and the algorithm terminates.

3. Find $\gcd(a_i, d)$ by Algorithm 5.2.1.
   Set $d \leftarrow \gcd(a_i, d)$ and $i \leftarrow i - 1$. Go to step 2. ♦

The algorithm works by repeatedly using facts (4) and (7) of Lemma 5.2.2. Suppose, for instance, we want to find the gcd d of four numbers a_1, a_2, a_3, a_4. Applying (7) twice, we get

$$\begin{aligned}
d &= \gcd(a_1, a_2, a_3, a_4) \\
  &= \gcd(a_1, \gcd(a_2, a_3, a_4)) \\
  &= \gcd(a_1, \gcd(a_2, \gcd(a_3, a_4))).
\end{aligned}$$

If $a_4 = 1$, then $d = 1$ by (4). Otherwise compute $\gcd(a_3, a_4)$. If $\gcd(a_3, a_4) = 1$, then $\gcd(a_2, \gcd(a_3, a_4)) = 1$, and hence $d = 1$. If $\gcd(a_3, a_4) \neq 1$, compute $\gcd(a_2, \gcd(a_3, a_4))$. If that gcd is 1, then $d = 1$. Otherwise compute $\gcd(a_1, \gcd(a_2, \gcd(a_3, a_4)))$ to get d. For a numerical example, consider $\gcd(99, -105, 210, 300)$. Since

$300 \neq 1$, find $\gcd(210, 300) = 30$. Since $30 \neq 1$, find $\gcd(-105, 30) = 15$. Since $15 \neq 1$, find $\gcd(99, 15) = 3$ which is the gcd of the four numbers.

5.3. SINGLE EQUATION IN TWO VARIABLES

Let x, y denote integer variables and a, b, c integer constants such that a, b are not both zero. In this section we will study the linear diophantine equation in two variables

$$ax + by = c. \tag{1}$$

Let $d = \gcd(a, b)$. We will show that the associated equations

$$ax + by = 0 \tag{2}$$
and
$$ax + by = d \tag{3}$$

always have solutions and that in case (1) has a solution, the general solution to (1) can be obtained by combining the general solution to (2) with any particular solution to (3).

Lemma 5.3.1. Let a, b denote integers, not both zero, and let $d = \gcd(a, b)$. The general solution to the equation

$$ax + by = 0 \tag{2}$$
is given by
$$(x, y) = (-b't, a't)$$

where $a' = a/d$, $b' = b/d$, and t is an arbitrary integer.

PROOF. Direct computation shows that $x = -b't$, $y = a't$ satisfy the equation for any integer t.

Now let (x, y) denote any solution. We have

$$ax = -by, \quad \text{or} \quad (a/d)x = -(b/d)y, \quad \text{i.e.,} \quad a'x = -b'y.$$

Since the integers a' and b' are relatively prime (Lemma 5.2.1(9)), it follows that y is an integer multiple of a', i.e., there is an integer t such that $y = a't$. Substituting for y, we get $x = -b't$, so that $(x, y) = (-b't, a't)$.   ♦

Algorithm 5.2.1 can be extended so that we can find a solution to equation (3) at the same time we compute $d \equiv \gcd(a, b)$.

Algorithm 5.3.1. (Extended Euclid's Algorithm).   Given two integers a, b, not both zero, this algorithm determines $d \equiv \gcd(a,b)$ and a particular solution $(x, y) = (x_0, y_0)$ to the equation

$$ax + by = d. \tag{3}$$

We manipulate 6 variables $x_1, y_1, c_1, x_2, y_2, c_2$ such that the relations

$$|a| \cdot x_1 + |b| \cdot y_1 = c_1 \tag{4}$$
$$|a| \cdot x_2 + |b| \cdot y_2 = c_2 \tag{5}$$

always hold. The algorithm stops when $c_2 = 0$ indicating that $c_1 = \gcd(a, b)$.

1. [Initialize.] Set $(x_1, y_1, c_1) \leftarrow (1, 0, |a|)$,
   $(x_2, y_2, c_2) \leftarrow (0, 1, |b|)$.

2. If $c_2 = 0$, then set

   $$(x_0, y_0, d) \leftarrow (\text{sig}(a)*x_1, \text{sig}(b)*y_1, c_1)$$

   and terminate the algorithm.

3. Set $q \leftarrow \lfloor c_1/c_2 \rfloor$.

4. [Subtract q times relation (5) from relation (4) and then interchange (4) and (5).]

Set

$$(t_1, t_2, t_3) \leftarrow (x_1, y_1, c_1) - q(x_2, y_2, c_2),$$
$$(x_1, y_1, c_1) \leftarrow (x_2, y_2, c_2),$$
$$(x_2, y_2, c_2) \leftarrow (t_1, t_2, t_3).$$

Go to step 2.

PROOF. If we focus on the right hand sides of relations (4) and (5), it becomes clear that Algorithm 5.2.1 is working on the integers $|a|, |b|$. The final value of c_1 is thus $d \equiv \gcd(a,b)$. This algorithm does a little more: The final values of x_1, y_1 satisfy

$$|a| \cdot x_1 + |b| \cdot y_1 = d,$$

and hence, after accounting for the signs of a, b in step 2, we see that $(x, y) = (x_0, y_0)$ is a particular solution to equation (3). ◆

Remark 5.3.1. A lot of computation may be avoided by suppressing y_1, y_2, and t_2. At the end of the algorithm, after setting

$$(x_0, d) \leftarrow (\text{sig}(a)*x_1, c_1),$$

we can compute y_0 from the relation $y_0 = (d - ax_0)/b$.

Example 5.3.1. We will apply Algorithm 5.3.1 to compute $d = \gcd(10, -14)$ and a particular solution to the equation

$$10x - 14y = d.$$

The changes in the values of the important variables are tabulated below. The algorithm stops when c_2 becomes 0, and the final values of x_1, y_1, c_1 are 3, -2, 2, respectively. Since the coefficient of x in the equation is positive and the coefficient of y is negative, we get $(x_0, y_0, d) = (3, 2, 2)$. Thus, the gcd of 10 and -14 is 2, and $(x, y) = (3, 2)$ is a solution to the equation $10x - 14y = 2$.

Table 5.1. Steps of Algorithm 5.3.1 for Example 5.3.1.

x_1	y_1	c_1	x_2	y_2	c_2	q
1	0	10	0	1	14	0
0	1	14	1	0	10	1
1	0	10	−1	1	4	2
−1	1	4	3	−2	2	2
3	−2	2	−7	5	0	

Theorem 5.3.2. Let a, b, c denote integers such that a, b are not both zero, and let d = gcd(a, b). The diophantine equation

$$ax + by = c \tag{1}$$

has a solution iff d divides c. When a solution exists, the general solution is given by

$$\begin{aligned} x &= c'x_0 - b't \\ y &= c'y_0 + a't \end{aligned} \tag{6}$$

where (a′, b′, c′) = (a/d, b/d, c/d); (x_0, y_0) is any particular solution to the equation ax + by = d; and t an arbitrary integer.

PROOF. Since a, b are not both zero, we have d > 0. If there are integers x, y satisfying (1), then d would divide c, since d divides both a and b. Hence, if d does not divide c, equation (1) cannot have a solution.

Assume now that d does divide c. Let x_0, y_0 denote a pair of integers satisfying $ax_0 + by_0 = d$. (Algorithm 5.3.1 demonstrates that such pairs exist and shows how to find one.) We see by direct computaton that for any integer t, the formulas in (6) give a solution to equation (1):

$$\begin{aligned} ax + by &= c'(ax_0 + by_0) - (ab' - ba')t \\ &= c'd - (ab/d - ba/d)t \\ &= c. \end{aligned}$$

Now, let (x, y) denote an arbitrary solution to (1). To complete the proof, we must show that an integer t exists such that x, y can be expressed as in (6). Define

$$x' = x - c'x_0,$$
$$y' = y - c'y_0. \tag{7}$$

Since $ax' + by' = 0$, Lemma 5.3.1 guarantees the existence of an integer t such that

$$(x', y') = (-b't, a't).$$

Substituting for x', y' in (7) we can write x, y in the form of (6).

◆

Thus, using Algorithm 5.3.1 and Theorem 5.3.2, we can decide if a given diophantine equation in two variables has an integer solution, and then find all solutions when one exists. The following example shows how this method can be used in the context of the dependence problem:

Example 5.3.2. Consider the program

```
        do I = 0, 20
S:              A(9*I + 22) =  ···
T:                   ··· =  ··· A(6*I − 17) ···
        enddo
```

The two variables shown would cause statement T to be flow-dependent on statement S, if there is a solution (i, j) to the equation

$$9i - 6j = -39 \tag{1}$$

subject to the conditions

$$0 \le i \le 20, \quad 0 \le j \le 20, \quad \text{and} \quad i \le j,$$

i.e.,
$$0 \le i \le j \le 20. \tag{2}$$

Algorithm 5.3.1 gives us $\gcd(9, -6) = 3$ and a particular solution $(i, j) = (1, -1)$ to the equation

$$9i - 6j = 3.$$

By Theorem 5.3.2, the general solution to (1) is

$$(i, j) = (-13 + 2t, -13 + 3t).$$

where t is an arbitrary integer. Substituting for i, j in the inequalities (2), we get

$$0 \leq -13 + 2t \leq -13 + 3t \leq 20.$$

This yields $7 \leq t \leq 11$. Thus, the proposed dependence exists and the set of all associated iteration pairs is

$$\{(-13 + 2t, -13 + 3t): \ 7 \leq t \leq 11\}$$

or

$$\{(1, 8), (3, 11), (5, 14), (7, 17), (9, 20)\}.$$

5.4. SINGLE EQUATION IN MANY VARIABLES

Let $x_1, x_2, ..., x_n$ denote integer variables and $a_1, a_2, ..., a_n, c$ integer constants such that the a's are not all zero. Let d denote $\gcd(a_1, a_2, ..., a_n)$. Here we generalize the methods of the last section to the linear diophantine equation in n variables:

$$a_1x_1 + a_2x_2 + \cdots + a_nx_n = c. \tag{1}$$

There are two associated equations:

$$a_1x_1 + a_2x_2 + \cdots + a_nx_n = 0 \tag{2}$$

and

$$a_1x_1 + a_2x_2 + \cdots + a_nx_n = d. \tag{3}$$

As in the two variable case, equations (2) and (3) always have solutions, and (1) has a solution iff d divides c. Also, if a solution to (1) exists, the general solution is found by combining the general solution to (2) with a particular solution to (3). For this general case it is convenient to use matrix methods—some of the concepts used are described in the appendix after this chapter; for more details, consult a linear algebra text. Let

$$\mathbf{x} = (x_1, x_2,..., x_n), \quad \mathbf{A} = (a_1, a_2,..., a_n)^t, \quad \mathbf{D} = (d, 0,..., 0)^t.$$

In matrix notation, equation (1) can then be written as

$$\mathbf{x}\mathbf{A} = c.$$

The following algorithm finds the gcd d and an $n \times n$ unimodular matrix $\mathbf{U} = [u_{ij}]$ such that $\mathbf{U}\mathbf{A} = \mathbf{D}$. The first row of such a matrix is a particular solution to (3), since

$$u_{11}a_1 + u_{12}a_2 + \cdots + u_{1n}a_n = d.$$

Algorithm 5.4.1. (Generalization of Algorithm 5.3.1.) Let a_1, $a_2,..., a_n$, c denote integer constants such that the a's are not all zero. Let

$$\mathbf{A} = (a_1, a_2,..., a_n)^t.$$

This algorithm finds $d \equiv \gcd(a_1, a_2,..., a_n)$ and an $n \times n$ unimodular integer matrix $\mathbf{U} = [u_{ij}]$ such that $\mathbf{U}\mathbf{A} = \mathbf{D}$, where $\mathbf{D}$ is the matrix $(d, 0,..., 0)^t$.

We are applying to $\mathbf{A}$ a reduction procedure (similar to Gauss-Jordan) for integer matrices. Let $\mathbf{I}$ denote the $n \times n$ identity matrix. The main idea here is to apply a suitable (finite) sequence of elementary row operations (as defined in the appendix) to $\mathbf{A}$ until rows 2 through n are zero. The same exact sequence of operations applied to $\mathbf{I}$ yields the matrix $\mathbf{U}$. This is done by augmenting $\mathbf{I}$ with $\mathbf{A}$ to form the $n \times (n + 1)$ matrix $(\mathbf{I}, \mathbf{A})$, and then transforming $(\mathbf{I}, \mathbf{A})$ by repeated applications of elementary row operations using column $(n + 1)$, until that column has a zero in each of the rows from 2 through n.

1. [Initialize.] Set $U \leftarrow I$, $D \leftarrow A$, and $i \leftarrow n$.
   (We will denote the elements of D by $d_1, d_2, ..., d_n$.)

2. [Done?] If $i = 1$, go to step 6.

3. If $d_i = 0$, set $i \leftarrow i - 1$ and go to step 2.

4. [Work on rows i, i–1.]   Set $q \leftarrow \lfloor |d_{i-1}| / |d_i| \rfloor$.
   If $q = 0$, go to step 5. Otherwise, set $s \leftarrow sig(d_{i-1} / d_i)$. Subtract
   sq times row i from row $(i - 1)$ in the augmented matrix
   (U, D). (In other words, subtract sq times row i from row
   $(i - 1)$ in the matrix U, and subtract sq times row i from row
   $(i - 1)$ in the matrix D.)

5. Interchange rows i and $(i - 1)$ in (U, D), (i.e., interchange rows
   i and $(i - 1)$ in both U and D). Go to step 3.

6. Now D has a zero in each of the rows from 2 through n. If $d_1 <$
   0, multiply the first row of (U, D) by -1. Set $d \leftarrow d_1$, and terminate the algorithm.

PROOF. The algorithm starts with the $n \times (n + 1)$ matrix $(U, D) =$
(I, A) and performs a finite sequence of elementary row operations on it. By Lemma A.3 in the appendix, at any point in the
algorithm the current value of (U, D) is given by

$$(U, D) = U'\cdot(I, A)$$

where U' is some $n \times n$ unimodular integer matrix. This implies
$U = U'I$ and $D = U'A$, so that $U' = U$ and $UA = D$. Thus, at any
point U is a unimodular integer matrix and $UA = D$.

When the algorithm stops, D has the form $D = (d, 0, ..., 0)^t$,
where $d > 0$. All we need to prove now is that $gcd(a_1, a_2, ..., a_n)$ is
given by d. The first scalar equation in $UA = D$ is

$$u_{11}a_1 + u_{12}a_2 + \cdots + u_{1n}a_n = d.$$

This shows that any common divisor of a_1, a_2,..., a_n divides d. On the other hand, U being a unimodular integer matrix, U^{-1} exists and is an integer matrix (Lemma A.1). Using the relation

$$A = U^{-1} \cdot (d, 0,..., 0)^t$$

and letting $U^{-1} = [v_{ij}]$, we get $a_i = v_{i1}d$ for $1 \le i \le n$. Since each v_{i1} is an integer, d is a common divisor of a_1, a_2,..., a_n. Hence d = $\gcd(a_1, a_2,..., a_n)$. ♦

Remark 5.4.1. A lot of computation may be avoided if we note that during the row operations, certain elements of U never get changed. In fact, when rows i and $(i - 1)$ are being processed, the first $(i - 2)$ elements in each row remain equal to 0, $(n \ge i \ge 2)$.

After a unimodular matrix U with $UA = D$ has been obtained, we can easily compute the general solution to the linear diophantine equation $xA = c$ which is equation (1) in matrix form. First, we get the general solution to the homogeneous equation $xA = 0$:

Lemma 5.4.1. Let a_1, a_2,..., a_n denote integers, not all zero. Let d = $\gcd(a_1, a_2,..., a_n)$, $A = (a_1, a_2,..., a_n)^t$, $D = (d, 0,..., 0)^t$. Let U denote any $n \times n$ unimodular integer matrix satisfying the condition $UA = D$. Then the general solution to the linear diophantine equation

$$a_1x_1 + a_2x_2 + \cdots + a_nx_n = 0 \tag{2}$$

is given by the formula

$$(x_1, x_2,..., x_n) = (0, t_2, t_3,..., t_n) \cdot U \tag{4}$$

where t_2, t_3,..., t_n are arbitrary integers.

PROOF. Since $a_1, a_2,..., a_n$ are not all zero, $d = \gcd(a_1, a_2,..., a_n) > 0$. For arbitrary integers $t_2, t_3,..., t_n$, (4) gives an integer solution to (2), since

$$\begin{aligned}
a_1x_1 + a_2x_2 + \cdots + a_nx_n &= (x_1, x_2,..., x_n)\cdot(a_1, a_2,..., a_n)^t \\
&= (0, t_2, t_3,..., t_n)\cdot U\cdot A \\
&= (0, t_2, t_3,..., t_n)\cdot(d, 0,..., 0)^t \\
&= 0.
\end{aligned}$$

It remains to be shown that all integer solutions to (2) are included in the formula (4). Let S denote the set of all *real* solutions to (2), i.e.,

$$S = \{x \in \mathbf{R}^n: xA = 0\}.$$

Clearly S is a vector subspace of $\mathbf{R}^n$, since if x and y are two solutions and α any real number, then $x + y$ and αx are also solutions. Now denote the ith row of the matrix U by u_i, $(1 \le i \le n)$. The relation $UA = D$ implies that rows u_2 through u_n satisfy $u_iA = 0$ and hence are in S. Since U is nonsingular, the vectors $u_2, u_3,...,u_n$ are linearly independent. Thus, $\dim(S)$ is at least $n - 1$. If this dimension were n, S would be all of $\mathbf{R}^n$ which is impossible, since $u_1A = d > 0$ and therefore u_1 is not in S. So, $\dim(S) = n - 1$. This means that the $n - 1$ linearly independent vectors $u_2, u_3,..., u_n$ form a basis of S. If $(x_1, x_2,..., x_n)$ is any solution to (2), i.e., any vector in S, there are *real* constants $t_2, t_3,..., t_n$ such that

$$(x_1, x_2,..., x_n) = t_2u_2 + t_3u_3 + \cdots + t_nu_n$$

or

$$(x_1, x_2,..., x_n) = (0, t_2, t_3,..., t_n)\cdot U.$$

If $(x_1, x_2,..., x_n)$ is an integer solution, then these t_i's must also be integers, since $(0, t_2, t_3,..., t_n) = (x_1, x_2,..., x_n)\cdot U^{-1}$ and U^{-1} is an integer matrix (Lemma A.1). This completes the proof. ♦

Theorem 5.4.2. Let $a_1, a_2,..., a_n$, c denote integers such that the a_i's are not all zero, and let $d = \gcd(a_1, a_2,..., a_n)$. The linear diophantine equation

$$a_1x_1 + a_2x_2 + \cdots + a_nx_n = c \qquad (1)$$

has a solution iff d divides c.

Suppose d divides c. Let

$$c' = c/d, \quad A = (a_1, a_2,..., a_n)^t, \quad D = (d, 0,..., 0)^t,$$

and U any $n \times n$ unimodular integer matrix satisfying $UA = D$. The general solution to (1) is then given by the formula

$$(x_1, x_2,..., x_n) = (c', t_2, t_3,..., t_n) \cdot U \qquad (5)$$

where $t_2, t_3,..., t_n$ are arbitrary integers.

PROOF. Since $a_1, a_2,..., a_n$ are not all zero, $d = \gcd(a_1, a_2,..., a_n) > 0$. If there is an (integer) solution $x_1, x_2,..., x_n$ to (1), then d must divide c, since d divides $a_1, a_2,..., a_n$.

Assume now that d does divide c. If $t_2, t_3,..., t_n$ denote arbitrary integers, then (5) gives a solution to (1), since

$$\begin{aligned}
a_1x_1 + a_2x_2 + \cdots + a_nx_n &= (x_1, x_2,..., x_n) \cdot (a_1, a_2,..., a_n)^t \\
&= (c', t_2, t_3,..., t_n) \cdot U \cdot A \\
&= (c', t_2, t_3,..., t_n) \cdot (d, 0,..., 0)^t \\
&= c'd = c.
\end{aligned}$$

We need to prove that an arbitrary solution $x = (x_1, x_2,..., x_n)$ to (1) can be obtained from the formula (5). Direct computation shows that $(x - c'u_1)$, where u_1 denotes the first row of the matrix U, is a solution to the homogeneous equation (2):

$$(x - c'u_1)A = xA - c'u_1A = c - c'd = c - c = 0.$$

By Lemma 5.4.1, there exist integers $t_2, t_3,..., t_n$ such that

$$\mathbf{x} - c'\mathbf{u}_1 = (0, t_2, t_3,..., t_n) \cdot \mathbf{U}$$

or
$$\mathbf{x} = (c', t_2, t_3,..., t_n) \cdot \mathbf{U},$$

so that $\mathbf{x}$ is included in (5).   ◆

Remark 5.4.2.

1. If one of the coefficients, say a_1, is 1, we can solve the equation very easily:

$$x_1 = c - a_2 t_2 - a_3 t_3 - \cdots - a_n t_n$$
$$x_i = t_i. \qquad\qquad (2 \leq i \leq n)$$

2. In view of the Remark 5.4.1, the final version of U will have a 0 in the elements u_{rs}, where $3 \leq r \leq n$ and $1 \leq s \leq r - 2$. Thus, the expressions defined by the formula giving the solutions in equation (5) are of the form

$$
\begin{aligned}
x_1 &= \alpha_{10} + \alpha_{12} t_2 + \alpha_{13} t_3 + \cdots + \alpha_{1n} t_n \\
x_2 &= \alpha_{20} + \alpha_{22} t_2 + \alpha_{23} t_3 + \cdots + \alpha_{2n} t_n \\
x_3 &= \alpha_{30} \qquad\qquad\quad + \alpha_{33} t_3 + \cdots + \alpha_{3n} t_n \\
&\;\;\vdots \\
x_n &= \alpha_{n0} \qquad\qquad\qquad\qquad\qquad + \alpha_{nn} t_n
\end{aligned}
$$

where the α's are constant integers and the t's are variables that can take any integer values.

Example 5.4.1. Consider the program

$$\textbf{do } I_1 = 1, 100$$
$$\qquad \textbf{do } I_2 = 1, 100$$

S: $\qquad\qquad A(I_1 + 2*I_2 - 3) = \cdots$

T: $\qquad\qquad A(-I_1 + 4*I_2 + 8) = \cdots$

$$\qquad \textbf{enddo}$$
$$\textbf{enddo}$$

In order that statement T may be output-dependent on statement S at level 2, there must be an integer solution to the equation

$$i_1 + 2i_2 - 3 = -j_1 + 4j_2 + 8$$

subject to the conditions

$$1 \le i_1 \le 100, \quad 1 \le i_2 \le 100,$$
$$1 \le j_1 \le 100, \quad 1 \le j_2 \le 100,$$
$$i_1 = j_1, \quad i_2 < j_2.$$

Using $j_1 = i_1$ we rewrite the equation as

$$2i_1 + 2i_2 - 4j_2 = 11.$$

This equation has no (integer) solution since $\gcd(2, 2, -4) = 2$ and 2 does not divide the right hand side. Hence T is not output-dependent on S at level 2. This particular testing method is known as the *gcd test*.

Note that when only the gcd of a set of numbers is needed, we can use Algorithm 5.2.2 instead of Algorithm 5.4.1.

Example 5.4.2. We will apply the methods of this section to the equation

$$2x_1 + 2x_2 - 3x_3 = 1. \tag{1}$$

The goal is to decide if the equation has a solution and then to find the general solution if solutions exist. Augmenting the 3×3 unit matrix $\mathbf{I}$ with the coefficient matrix $\mathbf{A} = (2, 2, -3)^t$, we get the 3×4 matrix $(\mathbf{I}, \mathbf{A})$ which is then transformed by Algorithm 5.4.1 until column 4 has the form $(d, 0, 0)^t$ with $d > 0$. The steps are shown below:

$$(\mathbf{I}, \mathbf{A}) = \begin{bmatrix} 1 & 0 & 0 & 2 \\ 0 & 1 & 0 & 2 \\ 0 & 0 & 1 & -3 \end{bmatrix}.$$

Interchange rows 2 and 3:
$$\begin{bmatrix} 1 & 0 & 0 & 2 \\ 0 & 0 & 1 & -3 \\ 0 & 1 & 0 & 2 \end{bmatrix}.$$

row 2 ← row 2 + row 3:
$$\begin{bmatrix} 1 & 0 & 0 & 2 \\ 0 & 1 & 1 & -1 \\ 0 & 1 & 0 & 2 \end{bmatrix}.$$

Interchange rows 2 and 3:
$$\begin{bmatrix} 1 & 0 & 0 & 2 \\ 0 & 1 & 0 & 2 \\ 0 & 1 & 1 & -1 \end{bmatrix}.$$

row 2 ← row 2 + 2*row 3:
$$\begin{bmatrix} 1 & 0 & 0 & 2 \\ 0 & 3 & 2 & 0 \\ 0 & 1 & 1 & -1 \end{bmatrix}.$$

Interchange rows 2 and 3:
$$\begin{bmatrix} 1 & 0 & 0 & 2 \\ 0 & 1 & 1 & -1 \\ 0 & 3 & 2 & 0 \end{bmatrix}.$$

row 1 ← row 1 + 2*row 2:
$$\begin{bmatrix} 1 & 2 & 2 & 0 \\ 0 & 1 & 1 & -1 \\ 0 & 3 & 2 & 0 \end{bmatrix}.$$

Interchange rows 1 and 2:
$$\begin{bmatrix} 0 & 1 & 1 & -1 \\ 1 & 2 & 2 & 0 \\ 0 & 3 & 2 & 0 \end{bmatrix}.$$

row 1 ← −1*row 1:
$$\begin{bmatrix} 0 & -1 & -1 & 1 \\ 1 & 2 & 2 & 0 \\ 0 & 3 & 2 & 0 \end{bmatrix}.$$

Thus, the matrices **U** and **D** of Algorithm 5.4.1 in this case are

$$U = \begin{bmatrix} 0 & -1 & -1 \\ 1 & 2 & 2 \\ 0 & 3 & 2 \end{bmatrix} \quad \text{and} \quad D = (1, 0, 0)^t.$$

The general solution to the homogeneous equation

$$2x_1 + 2x_2 - 3x_3 = 0$$

is given by

$$(x_1, x_2, x_3) = (0, t_2, t_3) \cdot U = (t_2, \ 2t_2 + 3t_3, \ 2t_2 + 2t_3)$$

where t_2, t_3 are arbitrary integer parameters. The gcd(2, 2, −3) is 1. Since 1 divides 1, equation (1) has integer solutions and the general solution is given by

$$(x_1, x_2, x_3) = (1, t_2, t_3) \cdot U = (t_2, \ -1 + 2t_2 + 3t_3, \ -1 + 2t_2 + 2t_3)$$

where t_2, t_3 are arbitrary integers. (Here, the c' of Theorem 5.4.2 is 1.)

5.5. SYSTEMS OF EQUATIONS

Finally, in this section we consider a general system of m linear diophantine equations in n integer variables:

$$\begin{aligned} a_{11}x_1 + a_{12}x_2 + \cdots + a_{1n}x_n &= c_1 \\ a_{21}x_1 + a_{22}x_2 + \cdots + a_{2n}x_n &= c_2 \\ &\vdots \\ a_{m1}x_1 + a_{m2}x_2 + \cdots + a_{mn}x_n &= c_m \end{aligned}$$

where the a's and the c's are all integers. We will extend the method developed in the last section for a single equation. Let C denote the $m \times 1$ matrix $(c_1, c_2, ..., c_m)^t$, and A the $n \times m$ matrix

$$\begin{bmatrix} a_{11} & a_{21} & \cdots & a_{m1} \\ a_{12} & a_{22} & \cdots & a_{m2} \\ \vdots & \vdots & \cdots & \vdots \\ a_{1n} & a_{2n} & \cdots & a_{mn} \end{bmatrix}.$$

The system of equations can then be written in the matrix form

$$\mathbf{x}\mathbf{A} = \mathbf{C}$$

where $\mathbf{x} = (x_1, x_2,..., x_n)$. (Note that $\mathbf{A} = [a_{ij}]^t$.)

The following algorithm shows how to find for a given $n \times m$ integer matrix $\mathbf{A}$, an $n \times n$ unimodular integer matrix $\mathbf{U}$ and an $n \times m$ echelon integer matrix $\mathbf{D}$ such that $\mathbf{U}\mathbf{A} = \mathbf{D}$:

Algorithm 5.5.1. (Generalization of Algorithm 5.4.1.) Given an $n \times m$ integer matrix $\mathbf{A}$ with no zero columns, this algorithm finds an $n \times n$ unimodular integer matrix $\mathbf{U} = [u_{ij}]$ and an $n \times m$ echelon integer matrix $\mathbf{D} = [d_{ij}]$ with $d_{11} > 0$, such that $\mathbf{U}\mathbf{A} = \mathbf{D}$. We apply a finite sequence of elementary row operations to $\mathbf{A}$ to transform it into an echelon matrix; the same sequence of operations performed on the $n \times n$ unit matrix $\mathbf{I}$ yields $\mathbf{U}$. This is done by augmenting $\mathbf{I}$ with $\mathbf{A}$ to get the $n \times (n + m)$ matrix $(\mathbf{I}, \mathbf{A})$, and then transforming $(\mathbf{I}, \mathbf{A})$ by repeated applications of elementary row operations using columns of $\mathbf{A}$, until $\mathbf{A}$ becomes an echelon matrix $\mathbf{D}$ with $d_{11} > 0$. This is a routine and straightforward generalization of Algorithm 5.4.1—we omit the details.

Note that the final value of d_{11} is the gcd of $a_{11}, a_{12},..., a_{1n}$, since $\mathbf{U}\mathbf{A} = \mathbf{D}$ implies

$$u_{11}a_{11} + u_{12}a_{12} + \cdots + u_{1n}a_{1n} = d_{11}$$

and $\mathbf{A} = \mathbf{U}^{-1}\mathbf{D}$ implies

$$a_{1i} = v_{i1}d_{11} \qquad\qquad (1 \le i \le n),$$

where $\mathbf{U}^{-1} = [v_{ij}]$. ◆

Theorem 5.5.1. Consider a system of m linear diophantine equations in n variables

$$a_{11}x_1 + a_{12}x_2 + \cdots + a_{1n}x_n = c_1$$
$$a_{21}x_1 + a_{22}x_2 + \cdots + a_{2n}x_n = c_2$$
$$\vdots$$
$$a_{m1}x_1 + a_{m2}x_2 + \cdots + a_{mn}x_n = c_m$$

or

$$\mathbf{x}\mathbf{A} = \mathbf{C},$$

where $\mathbf{x} = (x_1, x_2,..., x_n)$, $\mathbf{C} = (c_1, c_2,..., c_m)^t$, and

$$\mathbf{A} = \begin{bmatrix} a_{11} & a_{21} & \cdots & a_{m1} \\ a_{12} & a_{22} & \cdots & a_{m2} \\ \vdots & \vdots & \cdots & \vdots \\ a_{1n} & a_{2n} & \cdots & a_{mn} \end{bmatrix},$$

the a's and c's being integer constants. Let $\mathbf{U}$ denote an $n \times n$ unimodular integer matrix and $\mathbf{D}$ an $n \times m$ echelon integer matrix such that $\mathbf{U}\mathbf{A} = \mathbf{D}$. If an $n \times 1$ integer matrix $\mathbf{T}$ exists satisfying $\mathbf{T}\mathbf{D} = \mathbf{C}$, then $\mathbf{x} = \mathbf{T}\mathbf{U}$ is a solution to the system. Conversely, if $\mathbf{x}$ is a solution, there must exist an $n \times n$ integer matrix $\mathbf{T}$ satisfying $\mathbf{T}\mathbf{D} = \mathbf{C}$ and $\mathbf{x} = \mathbf{T}\mathbf{U}$.

PROOF. Suppose first that there is an $n \times 1$ matrix $\mathbf{T}$ satisfying $\mathbf{T}\mathbf{D} = \mathbf{C}$. Then we have
$$(\mathbf{T}\mathbf{U})\mathbf{A} = \mathbf{T}(\mathbf{U}\mathbf{A}) = \mathbf{T}\mathbf{D} = \mathbf{C},$$

so that $\mathbf{x} = \mathbf{T}\mathbf{U}$ is a solution to the system.

To prove the second part, assume $\mathbf{x}$ is a solution to the system. Since $\mathbf{x}\mathbf{A} = \mathbf{C}$, it follows, in particular, that $\mathbf{x}$ is a solution to the single equation

$$a_{11}x_1 + a_{12}x_2 + \cdots + a_{1n}x_n = c_1.$$

The unimodular matrix $\mathbf{U}$ satisfies the relation

$$U \cdot (a_{11}, a_{12},..., u_{1n})^t = (d_{11}, 0,..., 0)$$

where $d_{11} = \gcd(a_{11}, a_{12},..., u_{1n})$. Theorem 5.4.2 then implies that an $n \times 1$ integer matrix T exists satisfying $x = TU$. Furthermore, we have

$$TD = T(UA) = (TU)A = xA = C.$$

This completes the proof.   ◆

Remark 5.5.1. Given a system $xA = C$ of linear diophantine equations, we first find a unimodular matrix U and an echelon matrix D by Algorithm 5.5.1 such that $UA = D$. The next step is to see if an integer matrix T exists satisfying $TD = C$. This is done by seeking a solution to the equations

$$(t_1, t_2,..., t_n) \cdot D = (c_1, c_2,..., c_m)^t.$$

Since D is an echelon matrix, these equations are particularly easy to solve. If the system is inconsistent or one of the t's turns out to be a noninteger, then the system of equations $xA = C$ has no (integer) solution. (See the example below.) Otherwise, the general solution will be given by $x = TU$. Suppose a solution exists. The number of undetermined integer parameters in the general solution is $(n - r)$, where r is the rank of the matrix A. This number is same as the number of zero rows in D. If $r = n$, there are no zero rows and we get a unique solution to $xA = C$. If $r = n - 1$, there is exactly one zero row in D and hence there is only one parameter in the solution to $xA = C$. These special cases are important in dependence tests, since inequalities involving a single or no unknown parameter are easy to solve. An interesting class of systems where r turns out to be n or $(n - 1)$ is described after Example 5.5.1.

Example 5.5.1. Let us check for possible flow-dependence of T on S at level 2, caused by the variables shown in the following program:

```
        do I₁ = 1, 100
           do I₂ = 1, 100
  S:          A(4*I₁ − 2*I₂ − 1, −I₁ − 2*I₂) = ⋯
  T:              ⋯ = ⋯  A(I₁ + 2*I₂ + 1, −2*I₁ + 1) ⋯
           enddo
        enddo
```

The equations to be solved are

$$4i_1 - 2i_2 - 1 = j_1 + 2j_2 + 1$$
$$-i_1 - 2i_2 \quad = -2j_1 + 1$$

and the constraints are

$$1 \le i_1 \le 100, \quad 1 \le i_2 \le 100,$$
$$1 \le j_1 \le 100, \quad 1 \le j_2 \le 100,$$
and
$$i_1 = j_1, \quad i_2 < j_2.$$

Using $j_1 = i_1$ we rewrite the equations in the form

$$3i_1 - 2i_2 - 2j_2 = 2$$
$$i_1 - 2i_2 \quad = 1.$$

The coefficient matrix A in this case is

$$\begin{bmatrix} 3 & 1 \\ -2 & -2 \\ -2 & 0 \end{bmatrix}.$$

Augmenting the 3×3 unit matrix with A we get the matrix

$$\begin{bmatrix} 1 & 0 & 0 & 3 & 1 \\ 0 & 1 & 0 & -2 & -2 \\ 0 & 0 & 1 & -2 & 0 \end{bmatrix}.$$

After Algorithm 5.5.1 works on it, this is changed into the matrix

$$\begin{bmatrix} 1 & 0 & 1 & 1 & 1 \\ 0 & 1 & -1 & 0 & -2 \\ 2 & 1 & 2 & 0 & 0 \end{bmatrix}.$$

The first 3 columns give the matrix **U** and the last 2 columns the matrix **D**. The equation **TD** = **C** becomes

$$(t_1, t_2, t_3) \cdot \begin{bmatrix} 1 & 1 \\ 0 & -2 \\ 0 & 0 \end{bmatrix} = (2, 1).$$

This gives $t_1 = 2$ and $t_1 - 2t_2 = 1$. The undetermined parameter is t_3, but there is no integer value for t_2. Hence the system of equations has no integer solution, and therefore the dependence of T on S does not exist.

Two equations in a system are said to be *directly connected*, if there is a variable whose coefficient in each equation is not zero. A system of m equations is *connected*, if the equations can be arranged in such a way that the ith and $(i + 1)^{st}$ equations are directly connected, $(1 \le i \le m - 1)$. Two systems are *disjoint* if no equation in one system is directly connected to any equation in the other system.

Corollary to Theorem 5.5.1. Let the system **xA** = **C** considered above be connected and such that each of the m individual equations has only one or two nonzero coefficients. Then, the general solution to the system, in case solutions exist, is either unique, or can be put in the form

$$x_j = \alpha_j + t\beta_j \qquad\qquad (j = 1, 2,..., n)$$

where the α_j's and β_j's are integer constants and t is an arbitrary integer parameter.

PROOF. In view of Remark 5.5.1, all we need to prove is that the rank r of **A** is either n or $(n - 1)$. We will briefly sketch a proof based on induction on the number of equations in the system. We count a variable iff its coefficient in at least one equation in the system is nonzero. Note that r is the number of 'independent' equations in the system. The corollary clearly holds for a single equation of the type under consideration. Suppose it holds for any system of m equations (of the same type). Let us add a new equation to a system of m equations with n variables and rank r. The new equation has one or two variables. But it may have at most one *new* variable, since it must be directly connected to an equation in the original system. No new variables means n remains the same. The new rank is either r or $(r + 1)$, but still less than or equal to n. The old value of $(n - r)$ was 0 or 1, and so must be the new value. One new variable means that the new equation must be independent of the original system, so that the rank definitely goes up by 1. Since n also increases to $(n + 1)$, the value of $(n - r)$ is unchanged: either 0 or 1. ◆

Remark 5.5.2. Suppose a given system can be broken up into N disjoint subsystems, such that for each subsystem we have $(n - r) = 0, 1$. Then, the general solution to such a system, in case it exists, can be expressed in terms of N integer parameters $t_1, t_2,..., t_N$. The solution has the form

$$x_j = \alpha_j + t_{\sigma(j)}\beta_j \qquad (j = 1, 2,..., n)$$

where $1 \leq \sigma(j) \leq N$ for each j. This would happen if a system could be broken up into subsystems each of which satisfies the conditions of the Corollary.

Example 5.5.2. Consider the system of equations

$$3x_1 - x_2 = -5$$
$$4x_1 - 2x_4 = -4$$
$$3x_3 + 2x_5 = 11$$

It can be broken up into two disjoint subsystems: one containing the first two equations and the other containing the third, such that each subsystem satisfies the conditions of the Corollary to Theorem 5.5.1. The solution to the whole system turns out to be

$$
\begin{aligned}
x_1 &= t_1 \\
x_2 &= 5 + 3t_1 \\
x_3 &= 11 - 2t_2 \\
x_4 &= 2 + 2t_1 \\
x_5 &= -11 + 3t_2
\end{aligned}
$$

involving two unknown parameters t_1 and t_2; we omit the details of computation.

APPENDIX TO CHAPTER 5

SOME CONCEPTS FROM MATRIX THEORY

Some of the definitions and results from matrix theory used in Chapter 5 are briefly discussed here. Unless otherwise stated, a matrix has real elements. When we want to emphasize that each element of a matrix is an integer, we will refer to it as an *integer* matrix. The reader familiar with Gauss-Jordan reduction will not find much here that is new. Some changes have been made so that division by a number may be avoided—we want to make sure that an integer matrix remains one even after it undergoes certain transformations.

The *transpose* of an $m \times n$ matrix $A = [a_{ij}]$ is the $n \times m$ matrix $[a_{ji}]$ denoted by A^t. An $m \times p$ matrix A can be *augmented* with an $m \times q$ matrix B to create an $m \times (p + q)$ matrix (A, B) whose first p columns are the columns of A and the last q columns are the columns of B. Thus, if

$$A = \begin{bmatrix} 1 & 2 & 0 \\ 0 & 0 & -1 \\ 0 & 5 & 9 \end{bmatrix} \quad \text{and} \quad B = \begin{bmatrix} 1 & 0 \\ 0 & 0 \\ 0 & 7 \end{bmatrix},$$

then

$$(A, B) = \begin{bmatrix} 1 & 2 & 0 & 1 & 0 \\ 0 & 0 & -1 & 0 & 0 \\ 0 & 5 & 9 & 0 & 7 \end{bmatrix}.$$

Note that $U \cdot (A, B) = (UA, UB)$ for any $m \times m$ matrix U.

An m × n *echelon* matrix has the following form:

1. For some k in $0 \leq k \leq m$, the last k rows consist entirely of zeros.

2. For $1 \leq i \leq m - k$, if the first nonzero element on row i lies in column j, then each element in column j after row i is zero.

3. The first nonzero elements in the rows are in an echelon form, i.e., if the first nonzero element in row 1 appears in column j_1, the first nonzero element in row 2 appears in column j_2, and so on, then

$$j_1 < j_2 < \cdots < j_{m-k}.$$

(Note that we do not require each first nonzero element to be a 1.) Some examples of echelon matrices are

$$\begin{bmatrix} 1 & 0 & 0 & 0 \\ 0 & 1 & 0 & 0 \\ 0 & 0 & 1 & 0 \\ 0 & 0 & 0 & 1 \end{bmatrix}, \begin{bmatrix} 5 & 2 & 3 \\ 0 & -1 & 0 \\ 0 & 0 & 3 \\ 0 & 0 & 0 \end{bmatrix}, \text{ and } \begin{bmatrix} 0 & 5 & 2 & 3 \\ 0 & 0 & -1 & 0 \\ 0 & 0 & 0 & 3 \\ 0 & 0 & 0 & 0 \end{bmatrix}.$$

Let **A** denote any n × n square matrix. Its determinant is written as $\det(\mathbf{A})$. We have $\det(\mathbf{A}^t) = \det(\mathbf{A})$. Matrix **A** is *singular* if $\det(\mathbf{A}) = 0$, *nonsingular* if $\det(\mathbf{A}) \neq 0$. The inverse $\mathbf{A}^{-1}$ of **A** exists iff **A** is nonsingular: for a nonsingular matrix $\mathbf{A} = [a_{ij}]$ we have $\mathbf{A}^{-1} = [A_{ji} / \det(\mathbf{A})]$, where A_{ij} is the cofactor of the element a_{ij}. (A_{ij} is $(-1)^{i+j}$ times the $(n - 1) \times (n - 1)$ determinant obtained by deleting the ith row and the jth column in $\det(\mathbf{A})$. Note that we need A_{ji} and not A_{ij} in $\mathbf{A}^{-1}$.)

When dealing with integer matrices, the operations of addition, subtraction, matrix multiplication, scalar multiplication by an integer, augmentation, and taking the transpose always result in integer matrices. But, the inverse of a nonsingular integer matrix is not always an integer matrix. This is where the concept of a unimodular matrix comes in. A square matrix **A** is *unimodular* if $\det(\mathbf{A}) = \pm 1$. The important properties of unimodular matrices we will need are listed below:

Lemma A.1.

1. A unimodular matrix is nonsingular. The inverse of a unimodular integer matrix is a unimodular integer matrix.

2. The product of two $n \times n$ unimodular matrices is an $n \times n$ unimodular matrix.

PROOF. Let A, B denote $n \times n$ unimodular matrices.

Since $\det(A) \neq 0$, matrix A is nonsingular. If A is an integer matrix, the cofactor of each element is an integer. Since $\det(A) = \pm 1$, the definition of A^{-1} implies that it is an integer matrix when A is an integer matrix. Also, we have $\det(A^{-1}) = 1/\det(A) = \pm 1$, so that A^{-1} is unimodular.

For the second part, simply note that

$$\det(AB) = \det(A) \cdot \det(B) = (\pm 1)(\pm 1) = \pm 1. \quad \blacklozenge$$

Remark A.1. Let $x = (x_1, x_2, ..., x_n)$ be a variable $n \times 1$ matrix, $A = [a_{ij}]$ a constant $n \times n$ matrix, and $C = (c_1, c_2, ..., c_n)$ a constant $n \times 1$ matrix. If A is nonsingular, the equation

$$xA = C$$

has a unique solution $x = CA^{-1}$. When A is a unimodular integer matrix and C an integer matrix, this solution is also an integer matrix.

For any n, the $n \times n$ unit matrix is unimodular. Other examples of unimodular matrices are provided by the so called elementary matrices. An *elementary matrix of type* 1 is obtained by replacing a 1 on the main diagonal of a unit matrix by -1. An *elementary matrix of type* 2 results if we interchange two columns of a unit matrix. Finally, an *elementary matrix of type* 3 is obtained by replacing a zero element in a unit matrix by a nonzero integer. Direct computation shows that the determinant of any such elementary matrix is ± 1. The three matrices

$$
E_1 = \begin{bmatrix} 1 & 0 & 0 & 0 \\ 0 & -1 & 0 & 0 \\ 0 & 0 & 1 & 0 \\ 0 & 0 & 0 & 1 \end{bmatrix}, \quad
E_2 = \begin{bmatrix} 1 & 0 & 0 & 0 \\ 0 & 0 & 0 & 1 \\ 0 & 0 & 1 & 0 \\ 0 & 1 & 0 & 0 \end{bmatrix},
$$

and
$$
E_3 = \begin{bmatrix} 1 & 0 & 0 & 3 \\ 0 & 1 & 0 & 0 \\ 0 & 0 & 1 & 0 \\ 0 & 0 & 0 & 1 \end{bmatrix}.
$$

are 4×4 elementary matrices of types 1, 2, and 3 respectively.

We consider now three types of elementary row operations on any matrix:

Type 1: multiply a row by -1,

Type 2: interchange two rows,

Type 3: replace a given row r by row r plus an integral multiple of another row s.

An elementary row operation can be performed easily with the help of an elementary matrix. This is the content of the following lemma whose proof we omit:

Lemma A.2. An elementary row operation of type k on an $n \times p$ matrix A can be accomplished by forming the product $E \cdot A$, where E is a suitable $n \times n$ elementary matrix of type k, (k = 1, 2, 3).

For example, for any 4×3 matrix

$$
A = \begin{bmatrix} a_{11} & a_{12} & a_{13} \\ a_{21} & a_{22} & a_{23} \\ a_{31} & a_{32} & a_{33} \\ a_{41} & a_{42} & a_{43} \end{bmatrix}
$$

we form the products

$$
E_1 \cdot A = \begin{bmatrix} a_{11} & a_{12} & a_{13} \\ -a_{21} & -a_{22} & -a_{23} \\ a_{31} & a_{32} & a_{33} \\ a_{41} & a_{42} & a_{43} \end{bmatrix}, \quad
E_2 \cdot A = \begin{bmatrix} a_{11} & a_{12} & a_{13} \\ a_{41} & a_{42} & a_{43} \\ a_{31} & a_{32} & a_{33} \\ a_{21} & a_{22} & a_{23} \end{bmatrix}
$$

and

$$E_3 \cdot A = \begin{bmatrix} a_{11} + 3a_{41} & a_{12} + 3a_{42} & a_{13} + 3a_{43} \\ a_{21} & a_{22} & a_{23} \\ a_{31} & a_{32} & a_{33} \\ a_{41} & a_{42} & a_{43} \end{bmatrix}$$

to multiply the second row by -1, interchange rows 2 and 4, and replace row 1 by [(row 1) + 3*(row 4)], respectively. (Here E_1, E_2, E_3 are the elementary matrices defined on the previous page.)

The total effect of a sequence of elementary row operations on a matrix is described below:

Lemma A.3. Applying a finite sequence of elementary row operations to a matrix is same as multiplyng the matrix on the left by a suitable unimodular integer matrix. Thus, if the original matrix is a unimodular integer matrix, so is the final matrix.

PROOF. Let A denote any $n \times p$ matrix. By Lemma A.2, performing an elementary row operation on the matrix is equivalent to multiplying it on the left by a suitable $n \times n$ elementary matrix. Thus, after m elementary row operations on A, the result is a matrix of the form

$$A' = E_m E_{m-1} \cdots E_2 E_1 A$$

where E_1, E_2,..., E_m are $n \times n$ elementary matrices. Since each elementary matrix is a unimodular integer matrix, so is their product $U = E_m E_{m-1} \cdots E_2 E_1$, (Lemma A.1). The final matrix is then $A' = UA$, where U is an $n \times n$ unimodular integer matrix. This implies that if A is a unimodular integer matrix, then so is A' (Lemma A.1). ◆

Example A.1. We will show how elementary operations are applied to a 3×3 matrix A to reduce it to the echelon form:

$$\mathbf{A} = \begin{bmatrix} 2 & 4 & 1 \\ 3 & 0 & 1 \\ 2 & 3 & 2 \end{bmatrix}.$$

row 2 ← row 2 − row 3:
$$\begin{bmatrix} 2 & 4 & 1 \\ 1 & -3 & -1 \\ 2 & 3 & 2 \end{bmatrix}.$$

Interchange rows 2, 3:
$$\begin{bmatrix} 2 & 4 & 1 \\ 2 & 3 & 2 \\ 1 & -3 & -1 \end{bmatrix}.$$

row 2 ← row 2 − 2*row 3:
$$\begin{bmatrix} 2 & 4 & 1 \\ 0 & 9 & 4 \\ 1 & -3 & -1 \end{bmatrix}.$$

Interchange rows 2 and 3:
$$\begin{bmatrix} 2 & 4 & 1 \\ 1 & -3 & -1 \\ 0 & 9 & 4 \end{bmatrix}.$$

row 1 ← row 1 − 2*row 2:
$$\begin{bmatrix} 0 & 10 & 3 \\ 1 & -3 & -1 \\ 0 & 9 & 4 \end{bmatrix}.$$

(Interchange rows 1 and 2)
$$\begin{bmatrix} 1 & -3 & -1 \\ 0 & 10 & 3 \\ 0 & 9 & 4 \end{bmatrix}.$$

row 2 ← row 2 − row 3:
$$\begin{bmatrix} 1 & -3 & -1 \\ 0 & 1 & -1 \\ 0 & 9 & 4 \end{bmatrix}.$$

Interchange rows 2 and 3:
$$\begin{bmatrix} 1 & -3 & -1 \\ 0 & 9 & 4 \\ 0 & 1 & -1 \end{bmatrix}.$$

row 2 ← row 2 – 9*row 3:
$$\begin{bmatrix} 1 & -3 & -1 \\ 0 & 0 & 13 \\ 0 & 1 & -1 \end{bmatrix}.$$

Interchange rows 2 and 3:
$$\begin{bmatrix} 1 & -3 & -1 \\ 0 & 1 & -1 \\ 0 & 0 & 13 \end{bmatrix}.$$

The 10 elementary operations used above are represented by the following 10 elementary matrices (in this order):

$$\begin{bmatrix} 1 & 0 & 0 \\ 0 & 1 & -1 \\ 0 & 0 & 1 \end{bmatrix}, \begin{bmatrix} 1 & 0 & 0 \\ 0 & 0 & 1 \\ 0 & 1 & 0 \end{bmatrix}, \begin{bmatrix} 1 & 0 & 0 \\ 0 & 1 & -2 \\ 0 & 0 & 1 \end{bmatrix}, \begin{bmatrix} 1 & 0 & 0 \\ 0 & 0 & 1 \\ 0 & 1 & 0 \end{bmatrix},$$

$$\begin{bmatrix} 1 & -2 & 0 \\ 0 & 1 & 0 \\ 0 & 0 & 1 \end{bmatrix}, \begin{bmatrix} 0 & 1 & 0 \\ 1 & 0 & 0 \\ 0 & 0 & 1 \end{bmatrix}, \begin{bmatrix} 1 & 0 & 0 \\ 0 & 1 & -1 \\ 0 & 0 & 1 \end{bmatrix}, \begin{bmatrix} 1 & 0 & 0 \\ 0 & 0 & 1 \\ 0 & 1 & 0 \end{bmatrix},$$

$$\begin{bmatrix} 1 & 0 & 0 \\ 0 & 1 & -9 \\ 0 & 0 & 1 \end{bmatrix}, \begin{bmatrix} 1 & 0 & 0 \\ 0 & 0 & 1 \\ 0 & 1 & 0 \end{bmatrix}.$$

If we take the product of these matrices in the reverse order (i.e., the last matrix is the first in sequence and the first matrix is in the rightmost position), then we get the matrix

$$\mathbf{U} = \begin{bmatrix} 0 & 1 & -1 \\ 1 & 0 & -1 \\ -9 & -2 & 12 \end{bmatrix}.$$

It is easy to verify that $\det(\mathbf{U}) = -1$ and that $\mathbf{UA}$ is equal to the final echelon matrix we computed. This matrix $\mathbf{U}$ is the unimodular matrix of Lemma A.3.

CHAPTER 6

DEPENDENCE TESTS

6.1. INTRODUCTION

We stated four versions of the linear dependence problem at the end of Chapter 3, and then spent the last two chapters developing tools needed to solve that problem. Through some of the informal examples on dependence tests, the reader has already been given a glimpse of what to expect in this chapter. The problem is always to solve a system of linear diophantine equations subject to a set of linear constraints. The equations and constraints may take certain forms based on the program and the characteristics of the particular dependence under consideration. There are two major types of dependence tests: exact and approximate. In an exact test, we actually find the general (integer) solution to the system of equations and test to see if a solution exists that fits all the constraints. In an approximate test, we check if there is an integer solution to the system or to each individual equation, and then test certain necessary conditions for the existence of a solution to the system or to each individual equation, subject to the constraints. As we saw in Chapter 5, there are a number of undetermined integer parameters in the general solution to a system of equations. If the number of parameters is 0 or 1, we may apply the exact test, since then the inequalities (constraints) can be easily solved. The approximate tests are always applicable, but from the point of view of accuracy, they should be applied only when an exact test is not available. Also, there are approximate tests with different levels of approximation and hybrid tests that are sometimes exact, sometimes approximate. In each testing algorithm, we show how to decide if a variable x of a statement S and a variable y of a statement T cause T to be dependent on S. It is always possible to extend each algorithm such that the possibility of y, x causing a dependence of S on T is also checked at the same time. This could result in some savings, since certain operations are common to both processes.

An exact test for a very important case, namely dependence caused by one-dimensional arrays in single loops, is discussed in Section 6.2. Section 6.3 describes an approximate test for one-dimensional array elements in an arbitrary loop nest, and that method is then extended to multidimensional arrays in the following section. The final section contains a number of general comments about dependence tests.

6.2. ONE-DIMENSIONAL ARRAYS, SINGLE LOOPS

Consider a loop of the form

$$L: \qquad \textbf{do } I = p, q, 1$$
$$\vdots$$
$$\textbf{enddo}$$

not contained in any other loop, where p, q are integer constants, and the body is a sequence of assignment statements. We will study dependence between these statements, caused by variables that are elements of one-dimensional arrays. The subscript in each element is assumed to be of the form $(a_0 + aI)$ where a_0, a are integer constants. If x denotes a variable of a statement S and y a variable of a statement T, then the type of dependence of T on S that (x, y) can cause depends on whether x, y are input or output variables of their respective satements. For example, if $x \in OUT(S)$ and $y \in IN(T)$, then we are looking for possible flow-dependence of T on S.

The following theorem is a single loop, one-dimensional version of Theorem 3.2.1.

Theorem 6.2.1. Let S, T denote any two statements in the loop L. Let x denote a variable of S and y a variable of T, such that at least one of them is the output variable of the corresponding statement. Suppose that $x \equiv A(a_0 + a*I)$ and $y \equiv A(b_0 + b*I)$, where A is a one-dimensional array and a, a_0, b, b_0 are integer constants. The variables (x, y) will cause a dependence of T on S, iff an (integer) solution exists to the diophantine equation

$$ai - bj = b_0 - a_0 \qquad (1)$$

satisfying the conditions

$$p \leq i \leq j \leq q \qquad \text{(for S < T)} \qquad (2)$$

or

$$p \leq i \leq j - 1 \leq q - 1 \qquad \text{(for T $\leq$ S).} \qquad (3)$$

PROOF. Suppose the variables (x, y) cause a dependence of T on S. Then there are iterations I = i and I = j of the loop L, such that the instance S(i) of S_p is executed before the instance T(j) of T, and the memory location $A(a_0 + ai)$ represented by $A(a_0 + a*I)$ in iteration I = i is same as the location $A(b_0 + bj)$ represented by $A(b_0 + b*I)$ in iteration I = j. Since the locations $A(a_0 + ai)$ and $A(b_0 + bj)$ are identical, we get

$$a_0 + ai = b_0 + bj,$$

i.e., (i, j) is a solution to equation (1).

When S appears lexically before T, the instance S(i) of S will be executed before the instance T(j) of T in serial execution of L, iff $i \leq j$. When T appears lexically before S, in order for the instance S(i) to be executed before the instance T(j), the iteration $I = i$ must strictly precede the iteration $I = j$, i.e., we must have $i \leq j - 1$. When S and T are identical, the same thing holds: $i \leq j - 1$. Also, since i, j denote iterations of the loop L, we must always have

$$p \leq i \leq q \quad \text{and} \quad p \leq j \leq q.$$

Combining these inequalities separately for the two cases $S < T$ and $T \leq S$, we see that (i, j) is a solution to equation (1) satisfying either (2) or (3). ♦

Dependence in this case means dependence with direction (vector) 1 or 0 for the case $S < T$, and dependence with direction 1 for the case $T \leq S$. The following two corollaries are useful when more detailed information about the dependence is needed.

Corollary 1.

1. The variables $A(a_0 + a*I)$ of S and $A(b_0 + b*I)$ of T cause a dependence of T on S with a direction vector of 1, iff an (integer) solution exists to the diophantine equation

$$ai - bj = b_0 - a_0$$

satisfying the conditions
$$p \leq i \leq j - 1 \leq q - 1.$$

2. Let $S < T$. The same variables cause a dependence of T on S with a direction vector of 0, only if
   either $a = b$, $a_0 = b_0$,
   or $a \neq b$, and $(b_0 - a_0)/(a - b)$ is an integer between p and q.

PROOF. Dependence of T on S with a direction vector of 1 means that iterations i, j in the proof of Theorem 6.2.1 satisfy $i < j$, i.e., $i \leq j - 1$. This proves part (1). Note that this part applies to both cases $S < T$ and $T \leq S$.

Dependence of T on S with a direction vector of 0 is possible only when $S < T$. Taking $j = i$ in the equation, we get

$$(a - b)i = b_0 - a_0.$$

If $a = b$, the equation degenerates into $b_0 - a_0 = 0$, so that we must have $a_0 = b_0$ for the dependence to hold. If $a \neq b$, then the unique solution $i = (b_0 - a_0)/(a - b)$ must be an integer between p and q.
♦

Corollary 2. Let the coefficients of I in the two subscript expressions be identical and nonzero, i.e., $a = b \neq 0$. The variables $A(a_0 + a*I)$ of S and $A(b_0 + a*I)$ of T cause a dependence of T on S, iff $(a_0 - b_0)/a$ is an integer satisfying

$$0 \leq (a_0 - b_0)/a \leq q - p, \qquad \text{for } S < T$$
$$\text{or} \qquad 1 \leq (a_0 - b_0)/a \leq q - p, \qquad \text{for } T \leq S.$$

Also, in case of dependence, there is a constant dependence distance of $(a_0 - b_0)/a$.

PROOF. Note that when $a = b \neq 0$, equation (1) of Theorem 6.2.1 becomes

$$j - i = (a_0 - b_0)/a.$$

The proof then follows from the fact that $(j - i)$ lies between 0 and $(q - p)$ for the case $S < T$, and between 1 and $(q - p)$ otherwise. ♦

Remark 6.2.1. Suppose $a \neq b$ and the variables x, y cause a dependence. In that case, the dependence distance would be a constant only if there is exactly one associated dependence pair. This would become clear after Algorithm 6.2.1 where formulas for minimum and maximum dependence distances are given.

To construct the dependence graph of the loop L, we systematically compare each pair of statements S, T in L. Given S, T, we consider each pair of variables (x, y) where x is a variable of S and y a variable of T, such that both are not input variables. Once the variables have been picked, we can test for the dependence of S on T as well as the dependence of T on S at the same time, and also for dependence with a direction vector of 0 or 1. However, to keep the following algorithm simple, only total dependence of T on S will be considered. As we have already remarked, the choice of the variables determines the types of the dependences being tested.

Algorithm 6.2.1. Let S, T denote two assignment statements in the loop L. Let x denote a variable of S and y a variable of T, such that either $x \in$ OUT(S), or $y \in$ OUT(T), or both. Assume we have $x \equiv A(a_0 + a*I)$ and $y \equiv A(b_0 + b*I)$ where A is a one-dimensional array and a_0, a, b_0, b are integer constants. This algorithm decides if the pair of variables (x, y) causes T to depend on S. We also find the set of associated iteration pairs, and the minimum and maximum distances associated with the dependence, in case the dependence exists.

1. Set $c \leftarrow (b_0 - a_0)$. We must solve the diophantine equation

$$ai - bj = c. \tag{1}$$

subject to the conditions

$$p \leq i \leq j \leq q \qquad \text{for } S < T, \tag{2}$$

or

$$p \leq i \leq j - 1 \leq q - 1 \quad \text{for } T \leq S. \tag{3}$$

2. Go to the proper case:

Case 2.1. $a = b = 0$.

The dependence $S \delta T$ exists iff $c = 0$, (i.e., $a_0 = b_0$). When $c = 0$, the set of associated iteration pairs is

$$\{(i, j): p \le i \le j \le q\} \qquad \text{for } S < T,$$

or

$$\{(i, j): p \le i \le j - 1 \le q - 1\} \qquad \text{for } T \le S.$$

The maximum dependence distance is $q - p$, and the minimum distance is 0 or 1 according as $S < T$ or $T \le S$. Terminate the algorithm.

Case 2.2. $a \ne 0, b = 0$.

If $S < T$ and c/a is an integer between p and q, then $S \delta T$ is true, the set of associated iteration pairs is $\{(c/a, j): c/a \le j \le q\}$, and the minimum and maximum dependence distances are 0 and $(q - c/a)$, respectively.

If $T \le S$ and c/a is an integer between p and $(q - 1)$, then $S \delta T$ is true, the set of associated iteration pairs is

$$\{(c/a, j): c/a + 1 \le j \le q\},$$

and the minimum and maximum dependence distances are 1 and $(q - c/a)$, respectively.

Otherwise there is no dependence. Terminate the algorithm.

Case 2.3. $a = 0, b \ne 0$.

If $S < T$ and $(-c/b)$ is an integer between p and q, then $S \delta T$ is true, the set of associated iteration pairs is

$$\{(i, -c/b): p \le i \le -c/b\},$$

and the minimum and maximum dependence distances are 0 and $(- c/b - p)$, respectively.

If $T \le S$ and $(-c/b)$ is an integer between $(p + 1)$ and q, then $S \delta T$ is true, the set of associated iteration pairs is

$$\{(i, -c/b): \; p \le i \le -c/b - 1\},$$

and the minimum and maximum dependence distances are 1 and $(-c/b - p)$, respectively.

Otherwise there is no dependence. Terminate the algorithm.

Case 2.4. $a = b \ne 0$

Set $k \leftarrow (-c/a)$. If $S < T$ and k is an integer lying between 0 and $(q - p)$, then $S \; \delta \; T$ holds, the set of associated iteration pairs is

$$\{(i, i + k): \; p \le i \le q - k\},$$

and there is a constant dependence distance of k. If $T \le S$ and k is an integer between 1 and $(q - p)$, then $S \; \delta \; T$ holds, the set of associated iteration pairs is

$$\{(i, i + k): \; p \le i \le q - k\},$$

and there is a constant dependence distance of k. Otherwise there is no dependence. Terminate the algorithm.

Case 2.5. $a \ne 0$, $b \ne 0$, and $a \ne b$.

2.5.1. By Algorithm 5.3.1, find $d = \gcd(a, b) > 0$ and a particular solution (i_0, j_0) to the equation $ai - bj = d$.

2.5.2. If d divides c, go to the next step. Otherwise, there is no dependence; terminate the algorithm.

2.5.3. Set
$$(a', b', c') \leftarrow (a/d, b/d, c/d),$$
$$(i_1, j_1) \leftarrow (c'i_0, c'j_0).$$

2.5.4. Set
$$e_1 \leftarrow (p - i_1)/b',$$
$$e_2 \leftarrow (q - j_1)/a',$$
and

$$e_3 \leftarrow (i_1 - j_1)/(a' - b') \qquad \text{if } S < T$$
$$e_3 \leftarrow (i_1 - j_1 + 1)/(a' - b') \quad \text{if } T \le S.$$

2.5.5. Label e_1 a lower bound of t if $b' > 0$, an upper bound if $b' < 0$. Label e_2 a lower bound of t if $a' < 0$, an upper bound if $a' > 0$. Label e_3 a lower bound of t if $a' > b'$, an upper bound if $a' < b'$. Note that there is always at least one lower and one upper bound.

Collect the lower bounds of t and the upper bounds of t from the set $\{e_1, e_2, e_3\}$. Let t_1 denote the ceiling of the largest lower bound and t_2 the floor of the smallest upper bound.

2.5.6. If $t_1 \le t_2$, then the dependence $S \, \delta \, T$ holds, the associated set of iteration pairs is

$$\{(i_1 + b't, j_1 + a't): t_1 \le t \le t_2\},$$

and the minimum associated dependence distance μ_1 and the maximum associated dependence distance μ_2 are given by

$$\mu_1 = j_1 - i_1 + (a' - b')t_1, \quad \mu_2 = j_1 - i_1 + (a' - b')t_2, \quad \text{if } a' > b',$$

or

$$\mu_1 = j_1 - i_1 + (a' - b')t_2, \quad \mu_2 = j_1 - i_1 + (a' - b')t_1, \quad \text{if } a' < b'.$$

If $t_1 > t_2$, there is no dependence. Terminate the algorithm.

PROOF. The cases 2.1 through 2.4 are trivial—to understand, one only needs to write down the simplified version of equation (1) in each case. We consider Case 2.5. By Theorem 5.3.2, the general solution to equation (1) is given by

$$(i, j) = (i_1 + b't, j_1 + a't).$$

Now i, j must satisfy

$$p \le i \le j \le q \qquad \text{for } S < T,$$

or

$$p \le i \le j - 1 \le q - 1 \qquad \text{for } T \le S.$$

After substitution and simplification, the inequalities in terms of t are

$$p - i_1 \leq b't, \quad a't \leq q - j_1, \quad i_1 - j_1 \leq (a' - b')t \qquad \text{for } S < T,$$

or

$$p - i_1 \leq b't, \quad a't \leq q - j_1, \quad i_1 - j_1 + 1 \leq (a' - b')t \qquad \text{for } T \leq S.$$

From these, we find the bounds of t (step 2.5.5). Since t is an integer, it must be greater than or equal to the ceiling of the largest lower bound, and less than or equal to the floor of the smallest upper bound. The rest of the algorithm is straightforward. ◆

Example 6.2.1. Consider again Example 1.2 from Chapter 1.

$$\begin{aligned}
&\textbf{do } I = 1, 100 \\
\text{T:} \quad &\qquad C(I) = A(3*I + 1) + 1 \\
\text{S:} \quad &\qquad A(2*I + 7) = B(I) - 3 \\
&\textbf{enddo}
\end{aligned}$$

The variables $A(2I + 7)$ and $A(3I + 1)$ may cause a flow-dependence of statement T on statement S. An instance $T(j)$ of T uses the value computed by an instance $S(i)$ of S, iff iteration $I = j$ comes after iteration $I = i$ (in serial execution), and the variables $A(2i + 7)$ and $A(3j + 1)$ are identical, i.e., iff $i < j$ and

$$2i + 7 = 3j + 1 \quad \text{or} \quad 2i - 3j = -6.$$

This is a linear diophantine equation in two variables. Since i, j are values of the index variable I, they must also satisfy

$$1 \leq i \leq 100 \quad \text{and} \quad 1 \leq j \leq 100.$$

The general solution to the equation is

$$(i, j) = (3t, 2 + 2t)$$

where t is any integer. Substituting for i, j in all the inequalities, we get

$$3t < 2 + 2t$$
$$1 \leq 3t \quad\quad \leq 100$$

and
$$1 \leq 2 + 2t \leq 100.$$

There is only one integer t, namely t = 1, that satisfies all these constraints simultaneously. Hence, the variables A(2I + 7) and A(3I + 1) do cause the dependence S δ^f T. The iterations I = 3 and I = 4 satisfy all conditions in the definition of dependence.

As we observed in Chapter 1, the same pair of variables could make statement S anti-dependent on statement T. The roles of i and j are reversed in that case.

Example 6.2.2.

```
      do I = 1, 100
S:        C(I) = A(3*I + 12) + 1
T:        A(3*I + 7) = B(I) - 3
      enddo
```

To test for antidependence of T on S, we need to solve the equation

$$3i - 3j = -5$$

under the constraints:

$$1 \leq i \leq j \leq 100.$$

There are no integrs i, j such that $i - j = -5/3$. Hence, T is not anti-dependent on S.

6.3. ONE-DIMENSIONAL ARRAYS

We will develop here an approximate dependence test for the case when the variables x, y of statements S, T are elements of a one-dimensional array A, and the loop nests have arbitrarily many loops. It is based on a simple set of necessary conditions for the existence of a solution to a linear diophantine equation in a given region. We will first study these conditions in a general setting, and then apply them to the dependence problem in particular. It was already shown in Section 4.1 how to get a necessary condition for the existence of a solution to an equation $f(x) = c$ in a region $\Re$, using bounds of f in $\Re$. The following lemma combines a restricted form of that condition with a result on diophantine equations:

Lemma 6.3.1. Let $c, a_1, a_2,..., a_n$ denote integers such that the a's are not all 0. The linear diophantine equation

$$a_1x_1 + a_2x_2 + \cdots + a_nx_n = c$$

has a solution in a nonempty region $\Re \subset \mathbf{Z}^n$, which is a finite combination of trapezoids, only if

1. $\gcd(a_1, a_2,..., a_n)$ divides c; and
2. $b_{low}(f, \Re) \leq c \leq b_{up}(f, \Re)$,

where f is the function defined by $f(\mathbf{x}) = a_1x_1 + a_2x_2 + \cdots + a_nx_n$, and b_{low}, b_{up} are the bounds considered in Chapter 4.

PROOF. Suppose the equation has a solution in $\Re$. The first part follows from Theorem 5.4.2. For the second part, note that there is at least one point $(x_1, x_2,..., x_n) \in \Re$ where $f(x_1, x_2,..., x_n) = c$, and hence c must lie within the bounds of f in $\Re$.   ◆

Part 1 of this lemma is usually called the *gcd test*. There will be a *generalized* gcd test later on for a system of equations. The gcd of a set of numbers is frequently 1, so that this test is not always very helpful. Part 2 is the source of a number of inequalities that are widely used in dependence analysis; we have stated most of them in this book, including some that have never been published. The first inequality of this kind appeared in [Banerjee 1976]. That was extended and worked on by Wolfe [1982] and Allen & Kennedy [1987]. These inequalities have generally come to be known as *Banerjee's inequalities* (thanks to the authors cited above). They are all really the same inequality in a sense, and it would probably help the reader if we use the same name to describe them all.

It is shown in Chapter 4 how to compute the bounds b_{low}, b_{up} of a linear function in a rectangular or (more generally) in a trapezoidal region $\mathfrak{R}$. These bounds are often the extreme values of the function in the given region. We know also that if a region is not a trapezoid, but can be constructed from a finite number of trapezoids, using a finite number of operations of union and intersection, then Algorithm 4.3.1 and Lemma 4.1.2 may be applied repeatedly to compute these bounds.

Using the closed-form expressions for the bounds for two special cases of $\mathfrak{R}$, considered in Theorem 4.2.3 and Lemma 4.3.1, we get the following two corollaries:

Corollary 1. In Lemma 6.3.1, let $\mathfrak{R}$ denote a rectangle

$$\{(x_1, x_2,..., x_n) \in \mathbf{Z}^n \colon p_1 \le x_1 \le q_1, p_2 \le x_2 \le q_2,..., p_n \le x_n \le q_n\}.$$

If the equation

$$a_1x_1 + a_2x_2 + \cdots + a_nx_n = c$$

has a solution in $\mathfrak{R}$, then

1. $\gcd(a_1, a_2,..., a_n)$ divides c; and

2. $\displaystyle\sum_{k=1}^{n} (a_k^+ p_k - a_k^- q_k) \le c \le \sum_{k=1}^{n} (a_k^+ q_k - a_k^- p_k).$

Corollary 2. Let $\mathfrak{R}$ denote the triangle

$$\{(x, y): \ 0 \le x \le q, \ 0 \le y \le x \} \text{ in } \mathbf{Z}^2.$$

If a, b, c are integers with a, b not both zero, then the equation

$$ax + by = c$$

has a solution in $\mathfrak{R}$, only if
   1. gcd(a, b) divides c; and

   2. $-(a - b^-)^- q \le ax + by \le (a + b^+)^+ q.$

There is a particular type of equation for which the converse of each of the above corollaries also holds. We state the results without proofs; see [Banerjee 1976]. The basic idea here is as follows: Suppose we have an equation of the form

$$x_1 - x_2 = c$$

in a rectangle $\{(x_1, x_2): \ p_1 \le x \le q_1, \ p_2 \le x_2 \le q_2\}$. The function $f(x_1, x_2) = x_1 - x_2$ attains its minimum value at the point (p_1, q_2) and its maximum value at (q_1, p_2). It is not hard to see that it also assumes as its value each integer between the minimum and maximum values. This means that condition 2 will be sufficient for the existence of a solution. These ideas are valid in regions more general than rectangles or the triangles considered below. Note also that we may extend the corollaries to include equations which have coefficients of the form $\pm a$, where a is a nonzero integer.

Corollary 3. Let each nonzero coefficient a_k in the equation

$$a_1x_1 + a_2x_2 + \cdots + a_nx_n = c$$

be equal to ± 1, and let $\mathfrak{R}$ denote the rectangle of Corollary 1. Then, there is a solution to the equation in $\mathfrak{R}$, iff

$$\sum_{k=1}^{n} (a_k^+ p_k - a_k^- q_k) \leq c \leq \sum_{k=1}^{n} (a_k^+ q_k - a_k^- p_k).$$

Corollary 4. Suppose a, b $\in$ {0, 1, −1}, but not both of them are zero, and let $\Re$ denote the region of Corollary 2. Then the equation

$$ax + by = c$$

has a solution in $\Re$ iff

$$-(a - b^-)^- q \leq ax + by \leq (a + b^+)^+ q.$$

Lemma 6.3.1 is elaborated into an algorithm:

Algorithm 6.3.1. Given a linear diophantine equation

$$f(\mathbf{x}) \equiv a_1 x_1 + a_2 x_2 + \cdots + a_n x_n = c$$

in n variables, and a region $\Re \subset \mathbf{Z}^n$ which is a finite combination of trapezoids, this algorithm decides if there is a solution in $\Re$.

1. [The gcd Test.] By Algorithm 5.2.2, find $\gcd(a_1, a_2,..., a_n)$. If $\gcd(a_1, a_2,..., a_n)$ does not divide c, the equation has no solutions and the algorithm terminates.

2. If $\Re$ is a rectangle

$$\{(x_1, x_2,..., x_n) \in \mathbf{Z}^n: p_1 \leq x_1 \leq q_1, p_2 \leq x_2 \leq q_2,..., p_n \leq x_n \leq q_n\},$$

find the minimum value $b_{low}(f, \Re)$ and the maximum value $b_{up}(f, \Re)$ of f in $\Re$ from the formulas

$$b_{low}(f, \Re) = \sum_{k=1}^{n} (a_k^+ p_k - a_k^- q_k), \quad b_{up}(f, \Re) = \sum_{k=1}^{n} (a_k^+ q_k - a_k^- p_k).$$

Go to step 5.

3. If $\mathfrak{R}$ is a trapezoid, find by Algorithm 4.3.1, a lower bound $b_{low}(f, \mathfrak{R})$ and an upper bound $b_{up}(f, \mathfrak{R})$ of the function f in the region $\mathfrak{R}$. Otherwise, $\mathfrak{R}$ can be built up from trapezoids by a finite number of operations of union and intersection. Find the bounds of f in $\mathfrak{R}$ by using Algorithm 4.3.1 and Lemma 4.1.2.

4. [Banerjee's Inequality.]   If c does not satisfy

$$b_{low}(f, \mathfrak{R}) \leq c \leq b_{up}(f, \mathfrak{R})$$

then there is no solution in $\mathfrak{R}$. If c does lie in this range, there may or may not be a solution in $\mathfrak{R}$. Assume there is such a solution in that case.

We now adapt Algorithm 6.3.1 to the particular case of the linear dependence problem for one-dimensional arrays. The notation developed in chapters 3 and 4 is repeated here in part, for convenience:

We are considering two (not necessarily distinct) assignment statements S and T in the program. They determine three disjoint nests: the common nest **L** of loops containing both S and T, the nest **L**$_S$ of loops containing S but not T, and the nest **L**$_T$ of loops containing T but not S. There are e loops in **L**, m loops in **L** and **L**$_S$, and n loops all together in **L**, **L**$_S$, and **L**$_T$. These loops are labeled $L_1, L_2,..., L_n$ in such a way that

$$\begin{aligned}
\mathbf{L} &= (L_1, L_2,..., L_e) \\
\mathbf{L}_S &= (L_{e+1}, L_{e+2},..., L_m) \\
\mathbf{L}_T &= (L_{m+1}, L_{m+2},..., L_n).
\end{aligned}$$

For the loop L_k, the index variable is I_k, the lower limit p_k, and the upper limit q_k, (k = 1, 2,..., n). The index of the nest $(\mathbf{L}, \mathbf{L}_S)$ of all loops containing S is $(I_1, I_2,..., I_e, I_{e+1},..., I_m)$, and the index of the nest $(\mathbf{L}, \mathbf{L}_T)$ of all loops containing T is $(I_1, I_2,..., I_e, I_{m+1},..., I_n)$. There is a variable x of statement S and a variable y of statement T, such that at least one of them is the output variable of its statement. Assume that x, y are both elements of a one-dimensional array A, with linear subscripts:

$$x \equiv A(a_0 + a_1I_1 + \cdots + a_eI_e + a_{e+1}I_{e+1} + \cdots + a_mI_m)$$
$$y \equiv A(b_0 + b_1I_1 + \cdots + b_eI_e + b_{m+1}I_{m+1} + \cdots + b_nI_n),$$

where the coefficients are integer constants. We will first consider the more common case where the loop limits p_k and q_k are constants, and then look at the general linear case where they are linear functions of the relevant index variables.

By Corollary 2 to Theorem 3.2.2, x and y cause a dependence of statement T on statement S in the constant loop-limit case, iff there is an (integer) solution to the diophantine equation

$$(a_1i_1 - b_1j_1) + \cdots + (a_ei_e - b_ej_e) + a_{e+1}i_{e+1} + a_mi_m - b_{m+1}j_{m+1} - \cdots - b_nj_n$$
$$= b_0 - a_0,$$

satisfying the conditions:

$$p_k \leq i_k \leq q_k, \qquad (1 \leq k \leq m);$$
$$p_k \leq j_k \leq q_k, \qquad (1 \leq k \leq e \text{ and } m+1 \leq k \leq n);$$

and
$$i_k - j_k \begin{cases} < 0 & \text{if } s_k = 1 \\ = 0 & \text{if } s_k = 0 \\ > 0 & \text{if } s_k = -1 \end{cases}$$
$$(1 \leq k \leq e).$$

The number of integer variables in the system is $N = e + n - \Omega$, where Ω is the number of zeros in s.

The following algorithm, which is a special case of Algorithm 6.3.1, is a dependence test for one-dimensional arrays in the constant loop-limit case. (It will be assumed in the rest of the chapter that we are dealing with valid direction vectors and levels.)

Algorithm 6.3.2. Given a direction vector $\mathbf{s} = (s_1, s_2,..., s_e)$, this algorithm decides if the variables x of statement S and y of statement T cause a dependence of T on S with direction vector $\mathbf{s}$.

1. Partition the set $\{1, 2,..., e\}$ into four pairwise disjoint subsets:

$$P_0 = \{1 \le k \le e\colon s_k = 0\}$$
$$P_1 = \{1 \le k \le e\colon s_k = 1\}$$
$$P_{-1} = \{1 \le k \le e\colon s_k = -1\}$$
$$P_* = \{1 \le k \le e\colon s_k \text{ not specified}\}$$

2. [Set up the system.] Start with the $(n + e)$ variables $i_1, i_2,..., i_e,$ $i_{e+1},..., i_m, j_1, j_2,..., j_e, j_{m+1},..., j_n$. On this list cross out the variable j_k for each $k \in P_0$, so that finally there are $N = n + e - \Omega$ variables, where Ω is the number of elements of P_0. The diophantine equation to be solved is

$$\sum_{k \in P_0} (a_k - b_k)i_k + \sum_{k \in P_1} (a_k i_k - b_k j_k)$$

$$+ \sum_{k \in P_{-1}} (a_k i_k - b_k j_k) + \sum_{k \in P_*} (a_k i_k - b_k j_k) + \sum_{k=e+1}^{m} a_k i_k - \sum_{k=m+1}^{n} b_k j_k$$

$$= b_0 - a_0$$

2. [The gcd Test.] By Algorithm 5.2.2, find the gcd of the set consisting of the numbers

$$
\begin{array}{ll}
(a_k - b_k) & \text{for } k \in P_0, \\
a_k & \text{for } 1 \le k \le e, \text{ but } k \text{ not in } P_0, \\
a_k & \text{for } e + 1 \le k \le m, \\
b_k & \text{for } 1 \le k \le e, \text{ but } k \text{ not in } P_0, \text{ and} \\
b_k & \text{for } m + 1 \le k \le n.
\end{array}
$$

If this gcd does not divide c, the specified dependence does not exist and the algorithm terminates.

3. [Banerjee's Inequality.]   Check the inequalities:

$$\sum_{k \in P_0} \{-(a_k - b_k)^- (q_k - p_k) + (a_k - b_k)p_k\}$$

$$+ \sum_{k \in P_1} \{-(a_k^- + b_k)^+ (q_k - p_k - 1) + (a_k - b_k)p_k - b_k\}$$

$$+ \sum_{k \in P_{-1}} \{-(b_k^+ - a_k)^+ (q_k - p_k - 1) + (a_k - b_k)p_k + a_k\}$$

$$+ \sum_{k \in P_*} \{-(a_k^- + b_k^+) (q_k - p_k) + (a_k - b_k)p_k\}$$

$$+ \sum_{k=e+1}^{m} \{-a_k^- (q_k - p_k) + a_k p_k\} + \sum_{k=m+1}^{n} \{-b_k^+ (q_k - p_k) - b_k p_k\}$$

$$\leq (b_0 - a_0)$$

$$\sum_{k \in P_0} \{(a_k - b_k)^+ (q_k - p_k) + (a_k - b_k)p_k\}$$

$$+ \sum_{k \in P_1} \{(a_k^+ - b_k)^+ (q_k - p_k - 1) + (a_k - b_k)p_k - b_k\}$$

$$+ \sum_{k \in P_{-1}} \{(b_k^- + a_k)^+ (q_k - p_k - 1) + (a_k - b_k)p_k + a_k\}$$

$$+ \sum_{k \in P_*} \{(a_k^+ + b_k^-) (q_k - p_k) + (a_k - b_k)p_k\}$$

$$+ \sum_{k=e+1}^{m} \{a_k^+ (q_k - p_k) + a_k p_k\} + \sum_{k=m+1}^{n} \{b_k^- (q_k - p_k) - b_k p_k\}$$

If these inequalities do not hold, then x and y do not cause a dependence of T on S with direction vector **s**. If they do hold, then the algorithm offers no conclusions: there may or may not be dependence—assume there is.

PROOF. This is a special case of Algorithm 6.3.1. We need only explain step 3. The limits of the loop L_k being p_k, q_k, we must have

$$p_k \leq i_k \leq q_k$$
$$p_k \leq j_k \leq q_k, \qquad (1 \leq k \leq n).$$

Also, the specification of the particular direction vector s requires that

$$i_k = j_k \qquad \text{for } k \in P_0,$$
$$i_k \leq j_k - 1 \qquad \text{for } k \in P_1,$$
and
$$j_k \leq i_k - 1 \qquad \text{for } k \in P_{-1}.$$

These inequalities can be rewritten as follows:

$$0 \leq i_k - p_k \qquad \leq q_k - p_k, \qquad (k \in P_0);$$

$$0 \leq j_k - p_k - 1 \leq q_k - p_k - 1$$
$$0 \leq i_k - p_k \qquad \leq j_k - p_k - 1, \qquad (k \in P_1);$$

$$0 \leq i_k - p_k - 1 \leq q_k - p_k - 1$$
$$0 \leq j_k - p_k \qquad \leq i_k - p_k - 1, \qquad (k \in P_{-1});$$

$$0 \leq i_k - p_k \qquad \leq q_k - p_k$$
$$0 \leq j_k - p_k \qquad \leq q_k - p_k, \qquad (k \in P_*);$$

$$0 \leq i_k - p_k \qquad \leq q_k - p_k, \qquad (e + 1 \leq k \leq m);$$

$$0 \leq j_k - p_k \qquad \leq q_k - p_k, \qquad (m + 1 \leq k \leq n).$$

Note that each term in each summation on the left hand side of the equation in step 2 can be considered to be an independent function. For example, $(a_k - b_k)i_k$ is a function of i_k, for each $k \in P_0$, and $(a_k i_k - b_k j_k)$ is a function of the variables i_k, j_k for each $k \in P_1$, and so on. The domains of these functions are defined separately by the above inequalities. We compute the lower and upper bounds of each function using either Lemma 4.2.2 or Lemma 4.3.1. It helps to make slight changes in the variables so that each of them starts with zero. For example, for $k \in P_1$, we write

$$a_k i_k - b_k j_k = (- b_k)(j_k - p_k - 1) + a_k(i_k - p_k),$$

where

$$0 \le j_k - p_k - 1 \le q_k - p_k - 1$$

and

$$0 \le i_k - p_k \qquad \le j_k - p_k - 1.$$

Now apply Lemma 4.3.1.

The lower bound of $(b_0 - a_0)$ in step 3 is obtained by adding up all these lower bounds, and the upper bound is obtained by adding up all the upper bounds. ◆

Remark 6.3.1. The inequalities in step 3 get much simpler if the lower limit of each loop is 0 or 1, which is frequently the case in real programs.

If $p_k = 0$ for each k in $1 \le k \le n$, then the inequalities are

$$- \sum_{k \in P_0} (a_k - b_k)^- q_k \; - \sum_{k \in P_1} \{(a_k^- + b_k)^+ (q_k - 1) + b_k\}$$
$$+ \sum_{k \in P_{-1}} \{-(b_k^+ - a_k)^+ (q_k - 1) + a_k\} \; - \sum_{k \in P_*} (a_k^- + b_k^+) q_k$$
$$- \sum_{k=e+1}^{m} a_k^- q_k \; - \sum_{k=m+1}^{n} b_k^+ q_k$$

$$\le (b_0 - a_0)$$

$$\sum_{k \in P_0} (a_k - b_k)^+ q_k \; + \sum_{k \in P_1} \{(a_k^+ - b_k)^+ (q_k - 1) - b_k\}$$
$$+ \sum_{k \in P_{-1}} \{(b_k^- + a_k)^+ (q_k - 1) + a_k\} \; + \sum_{k \in P_*} (a_k^+ + b_k^-) q_k$$
$$+ \sum_{k=e+1}^{m} a_k^+ q_k \; + \sum_{k=m+1}^{n} b_k^- q_k$$

If $p_k = 1$ for each k in $1 \le k \le n$, then the inequalities are

$$\sum_{k \in P_0} \{-(a_k - b_k)^- (q_k - 1) + a_k - b_k\}$$

$$+ \sum_{k \in P_1} \{-(a_k^- + b_k)^+ (q_k - 2) + a_k - 2b_k\}$$

$$+ \sum_{k \in P_{-1}} \{-(b_k^+ - a_k)^+ (q_k - 2) + 2a_k - b_k\}$$

$$+ \sum_{k \in P_*} \{-(a_k^- + b_k^+) (q_k - 1) + a_k - b_k\}$$

$$+ \sum_{k=e+1}^{m} \{-a_k^- (q_k - 1) + a_k\} + \sum_{k=m+1}^{n} \{-b_k^+ (q_k - 1) - b_k\}$$

$$\leq (b_0 - a_0)$$

$$\sum_{k \in P_0} \{(a_k - b_k)^+ (q_k - 1) + a_k - b_k\}$$

$$+ \sum_{k \in P_1} \{(a_k^+ - b_k)^+ (q_k - 2) + a_k - 2b_k\}$$

$$+ \sum_{k \in P_{-1}} \{(b_k^- + a_k)^+ (q_k - 2) + 2a_k - b_k\}$$

$$+ \sum_{k \in P_*} \{(a_k^+ + b_k^-) (q_k - 1) + a_k - b_k\}$$

$$+ \sum_{k=e+1}^{m} \{a_k^+ (q_k - 1) + a_k\} + \sum_{k=m+1}^{n} \{b_k^- (q_k - 1) - b_k\}$$

Remark 6.3.2. The inequalities in step 3 of the algorithm can be stated in several different (but mathematically equivalent) forms, depending on the chosen forms of the inequalities involving the i's and the j's. We have chosen a form where the operations of taking the positive or negative values are few in number.

Remark 6.3.3. This algorithm does not provide an exact test for the existence of a solution in a given region, in general. When one of the conditions is not met, there can be no solution in $\Re$. But, when both conditions are met, a solution (at least an integer solution) in $\mathfrak{R}$ is not always guaranteed. If the conditions hold and each of the coefficients in the equation is from the set $\{0, 1, -1\}$, then the proposed dependence exists. We need to combine corollaries 3 and 4 to Lemma 6.3.1 for a proof of this; see [Banerjee 1976] for details.

Example 6.3.1.

$$
\begin{aligned}
&\textbf{do } I_1 = 1, 50 \\
&\quad \textbf{do } I_2 = -3, 20 \\
&\qquad \textbf{do } I_3 = 0, 30 \\
\text{S:} \qquad\quad & \qquad\quad A(3I_1 + 4I_2 - 3I_3 - 17) = \cdots \\
&\qquad \textbf{enddo} \\
&\qquad \textbf{do } I_4 = 2, 40 \\
\text{T:} \qquad\quad & \qquad\quad \cdots = \cdots A(-3I_1 + I_2 - 3I_4 + 37) \cdots \\
&\qquad \textbf{enddo} \\
&\quad \textbf{enddo} \\
&\textbf{enddo}
\end{aligned}
$$

Suppose we are testing for possible flow-dependence of T on S with direction vector $(1, 0)$. The equation to be solved is

$$3i_1 + 3j_1 + 3i_2 - 3i_3 + 3j_4 = 54 \qquad\qquad (1)$$

under the conditions

$$
\begin{aligned}
1 &\leq i_1 \leq 50 \\
1 &\leq j_1 \leq 50 \\
-3 &\leq i_2 \leq 20 \\
-3 &\leq j_2 \leq 20 \\
0 &\leq i_3 \leq 30 \\
2 &\leq j_4 \leq 40 \\
i_1 &\leq j_1 - 1.
\end{aligned}
\qquad\qquad (2)
$$

The gcd test is passed, since 3, the gcd of the coefficients of (1), divides 54. Computing the inequalities of Algorithm 6.3.2 we get

$$-84 \leq 54 \leq 159$$

which is true. So, the algorithm is not decisive and we would
assume that the proposed dependence exists. However, in this case
we are certain about the dependence, since (1) is really of the form

$$i_1 + j_1 + i_2 - i_3 + j_4 = 18$$

where each nonzero coefficient is ± 1 (Corollaries 3, 4 to Lemma
6.3.1 and Remark 6.3.3). Note that $(I_1, I_2, I_3) = (10, 0, 17)$ and
$(I_1, I_2, I_4) = (20, 0, 5)$ give one iteration pair associated with the
dependence; there are clearly many others.

   Algorithm 6.3.2 can be used to decide dependence with any
given direction vector, and hence dependence at any given level (in
the constant loop-limit case). We state below separately the conditions for dependence at a level, and for dependence with a direction vector useful in the study of loop interchange.

Theorem 6.3.2. When the loop limits are constant, the variables
x, y cause statement T to depend on statement S at a level u, only if

1. $\gcd\big((a_1 - b_1),..., (a_{u-1} - b_{u-1}), a_u,..., a_m, b_u,..., b_e, b_{m+1},..., b_n\big)$
divides $(b_0 - a_0)$, and

2. The following inequality holds:

$$\sum_{k=1}^{u-1} \{-(a_k - b_k)^- (q_k - p_k) + (a_k - b_k)p_k\}$$

$$+ \{-(a_u^- + b_u)^+ (q_u - p_u - 1) + (a_u - b_u)p_u - b_u\}$$

$$+ \sum_{k=u+1}^{e} \{-(a_k^- + b_k^+) (q_k - p_k) + (a_k - b_k)p_k\}$$

$$+ \sum_{k=e+1}^{m} \{-a_k^- (q_k - p_k) + a_k p_k\} + \sum_{k=m+1}^{n} \{-b_k^+ (q_k - p_k) - b_k p_k\}$$

$$\leq (b_0 - a_0)$$

$$\sum_{k=1}^{u-1} \{(a_k - b_k)^+ (q_k - p_k) + (a_k - b_k)p_k\}$$

$$+ \{(a_u^+ - b_u)^+ (q_u - p_u - 1) + (a_u - b_u)p_u - b_u\}$$

$$+ \sum_{k=u+1}^{e} \{(a_k^+ + b_k^-) (q_k - p_k) + (a_k - b_k)p_k\}$$

$$+ \sum_{k=e+1}^{m} \{a_k^+ (q_k - p_k) + a_k p_k\} + \sum_{k=m+1}^{n} \{b_k^- (q_k - p_k) - b_k p_k\}$$

PROOF. The proof follows from steps 2 and 3 of Algorithm 6.3.2, if we note that in this case the sets P_0, P_1, P_{-1}, P_* are as follows:

$$
\begin{aligned}
P_0 &= \{1, 2,..., u - 1\} \\
P_1 &= \{u\} \\
P_{-1} &= \varnothing \\
P_* &= \{u + 1, u + 2,..., e\}. \quad \blacklozenge
\end{aligned}
$$

When the lower limit is zero, the inequalities become much simpler:

Corollary 1. Let the lower limit of the loop L_k be 0 and the upper limit q_k, $(1 \leq k \leq n)$. Then the variables x, y cause statement T to depend on statement S at a level u, only if

1. $\gcd((a_1 - b_1),..., (a_{u-1} - b_{u-1}), a_u,..., a_m, b_u,..., b_e, b_{m+1},..., b_n)$ divides $(b_0 - a_0)$, and

2. $\quad - \sum_{k=1}^{u-1} (a_k - b_k)^- q_k - (a_u^- + b_u)^+ (q_u - 1) - b_u$

$$- \sum_{k=u+1}^{e} (a_k^- + b_k^+)q_k - \sum_{k=e+1}^{m} a_k^- q_k - \sum_{k=m+1}^{n} b_k^+ q_k$$

$$\leq \quad (b_0 - a_0)$$

$$\leq \sum_{k=1}^{u-1} (a_k - b_k)^+ q_k + (a_u^+ - b_u)^+ (q_u - 1) - b_u$$

$$+ \sum_{k=u+1}^{e} (a_k^+ + b_k^-)q_k + \sum_{k=e+1}^{m} a_k^+ q_k + \sum_{k=m+1}^{n} b_k^- q_k.$$

Corollary 2. When the lower limit p_k of loop L_k is 1, and the upper limit is a constant q_k, the variables x, y cause statement T to depend on statement S at a level u, only if

1. $\gcd((a_1 - b_1),...,(a_{u-1} - b_{u-1}), a_u,..., a_m, b_u,..., b_e, b_{m+1},..., b_n)$ divides $(b_0 - a_0)$, and

2. The following inequality holds:

$$\sum_{k=1}^{u-1} \{-(a_k - b_k)^- (q_k - 1) + a_k - b_k\}$$

$$+ \{-(a_u^- + b_u)^+ (q_u - 2) + a_u - 2b_u\}$$

$$+ \sum_{k=u+1}^{e} \{-(a_k^- + b_k^+)(q_k - 1) + a_k - b_k\}$$

$$+ \sum_{k=e+1}^{m} \{-a_k^- (q_k - 1) + a_k\} + \sum_{k=m+1}^{n} \{-b_k^+ (q_k - 1) - b_k\}$$

$$\leq (b_0 - a_0)$$

$$\sum_{k=1}^{u-1} \{(a_k - b_k)^+ (q_k - 1) + a_k - b_k\}$$

$$+ \{(a_u^+ - b_u)^+ (q_u - 2) + a_u - 2b_u\}$$

$$+ \sum_{k=u+1}^{e} \{(a_k^+ + b_k^-) (q_k - 1) + a_k - b_k\}$$

$$+ \sum_{k=e+1}^{m} \{a_k^+ (q_k - 1) + a_k\} + \sum_{k=m+1}^{n} \{b_k^- (q_k - 1) - b_k\}$$

Example 6.3.2. Consider

```
      do I₁ = 1, 100
        do I₂ = 1, 50
S:          A(3*I₁ + 2*I₂ + 15) = B(I₁,I₂) - 1
T:          A(-I₁ + 5*I₂) = C(I₁,I₁)
        enddo
      enddo
```

Statement T is output-dependent on statement S at level 2, iff there are iterations (i_1, i_2) and (j_1, j_2) such that both $S(i_1, i_2)$ and $T(j_1, j_2)$ compute values of the same variable, and $(i_1, i_2) <_2 (j_1, j_2)$. This holds iff the variables $A(3i_1 + 2i_2 + 15)$ and $A(-j_1 + 5j_2)$ are the same, and $i_1 = j_1$, $i_2 < j_2$. We have a linear diophantine equation

$$4i_1 + 2i_2 - 5j_2 = -15$$

with some constraints, namely

$$1 \le i_1 \le 100,$$
$$1 \le i_2 \le 50,$$
$$1 \le j_2 \le 50,$$

and
$$i_2 < j_2.$$

(The variable j_1 has been replaced by i_1.) The gcd test is passed, since $\gcd(4, 2, 5) = 1$ divides 15. The inequalities turn out to be

$$-244 \leq -15 \leq 392.$$

Since -15 lies between these two numbers, we would assume that the dependence under consideration does exist. In fact, it is easy to check that iterations $(i_1, i_2) = (4, 7)$ and $(j_1, j_2) = (4, 9)$ satisfy all requirements.

Theorem 6.3.3. With constant loop limits, the variables x, y cause statement T to depend on statement S with a direction vector of the form $(0, 0,..., 0, 1, -1, s_{u+2},..., s_e)$ with $(u - 1)$ leading zeros, only if

1. $\gcd\big((a_1 - b_1),..., (a_{u-1} - b_{u-1}), a_u,..., a_m, b_u,..., b_e, b_{m+1},..., b_n\big)$ divides $(b_0 - a_0)$, and

2. $\displaystyle\sum_{k=1}^{u-1} \{-(a_k - b_k)^- (q_k - p_k) + (a_k - b_k)p_k\}$

$\quad + \; \{-(a_u^- + b_u)^+ (q_u - p_u - 1) + (a_u - b_u)p_u - b_u\}$

$\quad + \; \{-(b_{u+1}^+ - a_{u+1})^+ (q_{u+1} - p_{u+1} - 1) + (a_{u+1} - b_{u+1})p_{u+1} + a_{u+1}\}$

$\quad + \; \displaystyle\sum_{k=u+2}^{e} \{-(a_k^- + b_k^+)(q_k - p_k) + (a_k - b_k)p_k\}$

$\quad + \; \displaystyle\sum_{k=e+1}^{m} \{-a_k^- (q_k - p_k) + a_k p_k\} + \sum_{k=m+1}^{n} \{-b_k^+ (q_k - p_k) - b_k p_k\}$

$\quad \leq (b_0 - a_0)$

$\quad \leq \; \displaystyle\sum_{k=1}^{u-1} \{(a_k - b_k)^+ (q_k - p_k) + (a_k - b_k)p_k\}$

$\quad + \; \{(a_u^+ - b_u)^+ (q_u - p_u - 1) + (a_u - b_u)p_u - b_u\}$

$\quad + \; \{-(b_{u+1}^- + a_{u+1})^+ (q_{u+1} - p_{u+1} - 1) + (a_{u+1} - b_{u+1})p_{u+1} + a_{u+1}\}$

$$+ \sum_{k=u+2}^{e} \{(a_k^+ + b_k^-)(q_k - p_k) + (a_k - b_k)p_k\}$$

$$+ \sum_{k=e+1}^{m} \{a_k^+ (q_k - p_k) + a_k p_k\} + \sum_{k=m+1}^{n} \{b_k^- (q_k - p_k) - b_k p_k\}$$

PROOF. The proof follows from steps 2 and 3 of Algorithm 6.3.2, if we note that in this case the sets P_0, P_1, P_{-1}, P_* are as follows:

$$P_0 = \{1, 2,..., u - 1\}$$
$$P_1 = \{u\}$$
$$P_{-1} = \{u + 1\}$$
$$P_* = \{u + 2, u + 3,..., e\}. \quad \blacklozenge$$

Corollary 1. Let the loop L_k have a lower limit of 0 and an upper limit of q_k, $(1 \leq k \leq n)$. Then the variables x, y cause statement T to depend on statement S with a direction vector of the form $(0, 0,..., 0, 1, -1, s_{u+2},..., s_e)$ with $(u - 1)$ leading zeros, only if

1. $\gcd((a_1 - b_1),..., (a_{u-1} - b_{u-1}), a_u,..., a_m, b_u,..., b_e, b_{m+1},..., b_n)$ divides $(b_0 - a_0)$, and

2. $\quad -\sum_{k=1}^{u-1} (a_k - b_k)^- q_k - (a_u^- + b_u)^+ (q_u - 1) - b_u$

$$\quad - (b_{u+1}^+ - a_{u+1})^+ (q_{u+1} - 1) + a_{u+1}$$

$$\quad - \sum_{k=u+2}^{e} (a_k^- + b_k^+)q_k - \sum_{k=e+1}^{m} a_k^- q_k - \sum_{k=m+1}^{n} b_k^+ q_k$$

$$\leq (b_0 - a_0)$$

$$\leq \sum_{k=1}^{u-1} (a_k - b_k)^+ q_k - (a_u^+ - b_u)^+ (q_u - 1) - b_u$$

$$- (b_{u+1}^- + a_{u+1})^+ (q_{u+1} - 1) + a_{u+1}$$

$$+ \sum_{k=u+2}^{e} (a_k^+ + b_k^-) q_k + \sum_{k=e+1}^{m} a_k^+ q_k + \sum_{k=m+1}^{n} b_k^- q_k$$

Corollary 2. If the lower limit p_k of each loop L_k is 1 and the upper limit is a constant q_k, then the variables x, y cause statement T to depend on statement S with a direction vector of the form $(0, 0,..., 0, 1, -1, s_{u+2},..., s_e)$ with $(u - 1)$ leading zeros, only if

1. $\gcd((a_1 - b_1),..., (a_{u-1} - b_{u-1}), a_u,..., a_m, b_u,..., b_e, b_{m+1},..., b_n)$ divides $(b_0 - a_0)$, and

2. $$\sum_{k=1}^{u-1} \{-(a_k - b_k)^- (q_k - 1) + a_k - b_k\}$$

$$+ \{-(a_u^- + b_u)^+ (q_u - 2) + a_u - 2b_u\}$$

$$+ \{-(b_{u+1}^+ - a_{u+1})^+ (q_{u+1} - 2) + 2a_{u+1} - b_{u+1}\}$$

$$+ \sum_{k=u+2}^{e} \{-(a_k^- + b_k^+)(q_k - 1) + a_k - b_k\}$$

$$+ \sum_{k=e+1}^{m} \{-a_k^- (q_k - 1) + a_k\} + \sum_{k=m+1}^{n} \{-b_k^+ (q_k - 1) - b_k\}$$

$$\leq (b_0 - a_0)$$

$$\leq \sum_{k=1}^{u-1} \{(a_k - b_k)^+ (q_k - 1) + a_k - b_k\}$$

$$+ \ \{(a_u^+ - b_u)^+ (q_u - 2) + a_u - 2b_u\}$$

$$+ \ \{-(b_{u+1}^- + a_{u+1})^+ (q_{u+1} - 2) + 2a_{u+1} - b_{u+1}\}$$

$$+ \ \sum_{k=u+2}^{e} \{(a_k^+ + b_k^-)(q_k - 1) + a_k - b_k\}$$

$$+ \ \sum_{k=e+1}^{m} \{a_k^+ (q_k - 1) + a_k\} \ + \ \sum_{k=m+1}^{n} \{b_k^- (q_k - 1) - b_k\}$$

When the loop limits are not constant, an algorithm similar to Algorithm 6.3.2 still works. Now the constraints are more complicated, and the region $\mathfrak{R}$ may not even be a trapezoid, although it can be expressed as a combination of trapezoids. We state in Theorem 6.3.3 the conditions for dependence at a level in this case; see Chapter 3 for notation. Similar conditions for dependence with a given direction vector exist, but are not considered here.

Theorem 6.3.4. The variables (x, y) cause a dependence of statement T on statement S at a level u, only if

1. $\gcd((a_1 - b_1),..., (a_{u-1} - b_{u-1}), a_u,..., a_m, b_u,..., b_e, b_{m+1},..., b_n)$ divides $(b_0 - a_0)$, and

2. $\qquad\qquad b_{low}(f, \mathfrak{R}) \leq b_0 - a_0 \leq b_{up}(f, \mathfrak{R}),$
   where

   $$f(i_1, i_2,..., i_{u-1}, i_u,..., i_m, j_u,..., j_e, j_{u+1},..., j_n)$$

   $$= \sum_{k=1}^{u-1} (a_k - b_k)i_k + (a_u i_u - b_u j_u) + \sum_{k=u+1}^{m} a_k i_k - \sum_{k=u+1}^{e} b_k j_k - \sum_{k=m+1}^{n} b_k j_k.$$

and $\mathfrak{R} \subset \mathbf{Z}^N$ is a trapezoid defined by the inequalities

$$p_{k0} + p_{k1}i_1 + \cdots + p_{k,k-1}i_{k-1} \leq i_k \leq q_{k0} + q_{k1}i_1 + \cdots + q_{k,k-1}i_{k-1},$$
$$(1 \leq k \leq u - 1);$$

$$p_{u0} + p_{u1}i_1 + \cdots + p_{u,u-1}i_{u-1}$$
$$\leq i_u$$
$$\leq (-1 + q_{u0}) + q_{u1}i_1 + \cdots + q_{u,u-1}i_{u-1};$$

$$i_u + 1 \leq j_u \leq q_{u0} + q_{u1}i_1 + \cdots + q_{u,u-1}i_{u-1};$$

$$p_{k0} + p_{k1}i_1 + \cdots + p_{k,k-1}i_{k-1} \leq i_k \leq q_{k0} + q_{k1}i_1 + \cdots + q_{k,k-1}i_{k-1},$$
$$(u + 1 \leq k \leq m);$$

$$p_{k0} + p_{k1}j_1 + \cdots + p_{k,k-1}j_{k-1} \leq j_k \leq q_{k0} + q_{k1}j_1 + \cdots + q_{k,k-1}j_{k-1},$$
$$(u + 1 \leq k \leq e, \ m + 1 \leq k \leq n).$$

Example 6.3.3. We can handle the so called triangular and trapezoidal loops using the methods of this theorem. Consider a loop of the form

```
        do I₁ = p₁, q₁
            do I₂ = p₂₀ + p₂₁I₁, q₂₀ + q₂₁I₁
S:              A(a₁₀ + a₁₁I₁ + a₁₂I₂) = ···
T:                  ··· = ··· A(b₁₀ + b₁₁I₁ + b₁₂I₂) ···
            enddo
        enddo
```

To test for dependence of T on S at level 1, we have to solve the equation

$$a_{11}i_1 - b_{11}j_1 + a_{12}i_2 - b_{12}j_2 = b_{10} - a_{10}$$

in the trapezoid

$$p_{10} \leq i_1 \leq q_{10} - 1$$
$$1 + i_1 \leq j_1 \leq q_{10} + q_{11}i_1$$
$$p_{20} + p_{21}i_1 \leq i_2 \leq q_{20} + q_{21}i_1$$
$$p_{20} + p_{21}j_1 \leq j_2 \leq q_{20} + q_{21}j_1.$$

We would compute the bounds b_{low} and b_{up} using Algorithm 4.3.1, and then use Algorithm 6.3.1.

The inequalities for direction vectors are usually more complicated. For example, to test for dependence of T on S with direction vector $(1, -1)$ in the loop

$$
\begin{aligned}
&\textbf{do } I_1 = 1, 100 \\
&\quad \textbf{do } I_2 = I_1, 50 \\
\text{S:} &\qquad A(I_1 - 2I_2 - 60) = \cdots \\
\text{T:} &\qquad \cdots = \cdots A(-I_1 - I_2 + 50) \cdots \\
&\quad \textbf{enddo} \\
&\textbf{enddo}
\end{aligned}
$$

the equation to be solved is

$$i_1 + j_1 - 2i_2 + j_2 = 110$$

in the trapezoid

$$
\begin{aligned}
1 &\leq i_1 \leq 99 \\
i_1 + 1 &\leq j_1 \leq 100 \\
i_1 &\leq i_2 \leq 50 \\
j_1 &\leq j_2 \leq i_2 - 1.
\end{aligned}
$$

We compute the bounds b_{low} and b_{up} of the function $f(i_1, j_1, i_2, j_2) = i_1 + j_1 - 2i_2 + j_2$ using Algorithm 4.3.1:

$$
\begin{aligned}
i_1 + j_1 - 2i_2 + j_2 &\geq i_1 + 2j_1 - 2i_2 \\
&\geq i_1 + 2j_1 - 100 \\
&\geq 3i_1 - 98 \\
&\geq -95 \\
&= b_{low}(f)
\end{aligned}
$$

and

$$
\begin{aligned}
i_1 + j_1 - 2i_2 + j_2 &\leq i_1 + j_1 - i_2 + 1 \\
&\leq j_1 + 1 \\
&\leq 101 \\
&= b_{up}(f)
\end{aligned}
$$

Since the right hand side of the equation does not lie between -95 and 101, statement T is not flow-dependent on statement S with direction vector $(1, -1)$.

6.4. GENERAL CASE

For the general linear dependence problem (Theorem 3.2.2), we have to decide if a system of equations has a solution satisfying a number of constraints. There are different ways of handling this problem with different levels of approximation. We will discuss below some of these methods. It is convenient to state the algorithms in a general setting. Their specialized versions dealing with dependence can be easily derived much the same way Algorithm 6.3.2 was derived from Algorithm 6.3.1.

One way to solve a system of equations subject to a system of constraints is to treat each equation separately:

Algorithm 6.4.1. Let $\Re$ denote a subset of $\mathbf{Z}^n$ that is either a rectangle, a trapezoid, or a region that can be built up from trapezoids by a finite number of operations of union and intersection. Given a system of m linear diophantine equations

$$f_r(\mathbf{x}) \equiv a_{r1}x_1 + a_{r2}x_2 + \cdots + a_{rn}x_n = c_r \qquad (1 \le r \le m)$$

in n variables, this algorithm decides if there is a solution to the system in $\Re$.

1. Set $r \leftarrow 1$.

2. By Algorithm 5.2.2, find $\gcd(a_{r1}, a_{r2}, ..., a_{rn})$. If this gcd does not divide c_r, the rth equation (and hence the system) has no solution and the algorithm terminates.

3. If $\Re$ is a rectangle

$\{(x_1, x_2,..., x_n) \in \mathbf{Z}^n: p_1 \le x_1 \le q_1, p_2 \le x_2 \le q_2,..., p_n \le x_n \le q_n\},$

find the minimum value $b_{low}(f_r, \Re)$ and the maximum value $b_{up}(f_r, \Re)$ of f_r in $\Re$ from the formulas

$$b_{low}(f_r, \Re) = \sum_{k=1}^{n} (a_{rk}^+ p_k - a_{rk}^- q_k), \quad b_{up}(f_r, \Re) = \sum_{k=1}^{n} (a_{rk}^+ q_k - a_{rk}^- p_k).$$

Go to step 5.

4. If $\Re$ is a trapezoid, find by Algorithm 4.3.1, a lower bound $b_{low}(f_r, \Re)$ and an upper bound $b_{up}(f_r, \Re)$ of the function f_r in the region $\Re$. Otherwise, $\Re$ can be built up from trapezoids by a finite number of operations of union and intersection. Find the bounds for f_r in $\Re$ by using Algorithm 4.3.1 and Lemma 4.1.2.

5. [Banerjee's Inequality.]   If c_r does not satisfy

$$b_{low}(f_r, \Re) \le c_r \le b_{up}(f_r, \Re),$$

then there is no solution to the rth equation (and hence to the system) in $\Re$ and the algorithm terminates.

6. Set $r \leftarrow r + 1$. If $r \le m$, go to step 2.

7. Assume the system has a solution in $\Re$ and terminate the algorithm.   ♦

Example 6.4.1.

```
        do I₁ = 0, 20
          do I₂ = 0, 20
S:            A(3I₁ − 2I₂ − 1,  4I₁ − 2I₂ − 4) = ···
T:            ··· = ··· A(2I₁ + 2I₂ + 1,  −3I₁ − 6I₂ + 3) ···
          enddo
        enddo
```

Test for possible flow-dependence of T on S at level 2. The equations are

$$i_1 - 2i_2 - 2j_2 = 2$$
$$7i_1 - 2i_2 + 6j_2 = 7$$

and the region $\Re$ is defined by

$$0 \leq i_1 \leq 20$$
$$0 \leq i_2 \leq 20$$
$$0 \leq j_2 \leq 20$$
$$i_2 \leq j_2 - 1.$$

Each equation passes the gcd test. The bounds for the left hand sides of the equations are

$$b_{low}(i_1 - 2i_2 - 2j_2) = -78, \qquad b_{up}(i_1 - 2i_2 - 2j_2) = 18;$$

and

$$b_{low}(7i_1 - 2i_2 + 6j_2) = 6, \qquad b_{up}(7i_1 - 2i_2 + 6j_2) = 260.$$

Thus the Banerjee inequality is also satisfied by each equation, and hence Algorithm 6.4.1 is not decisive. We will have to assume the proposed dependence.

The previous algorithm can be improved if we test for the existence of a solution (without constraints) to the system as a whole, and not separately to each equation. The new algorithm is based on the following theorem which combines Theorem 5.5.1 and Lemma 6.3.1:

Theorem 6.4.1. Consider a system of m linear diophantine equations

$$f_r(\mathbf{x}) \equiv a_{r1}x_1 + a_{r2}x_2 + \cdots + a_{rn}x_n = c_r \qquad (1 \leq r \leq m)$$

in n variables and a nonempty region $\Re \subset \mathbf{Z}^n$. Let A denote the $n \times m$ coefficient matrix $[a_{rk}]^t$, C the $m \times 1$ matrix $(c_1, c_2,..., c_m)^t$, U an $n \times n$ unimodular integer matrix and $\mathbf{D}$ an $n \times m$ echelon integer matrix, such that $\mathbf{UA} = \mathbf{D}$. Also, let $b_{low}(f_r, \Re)$ denote a lower bound and $b_{up}(f_r, \Re)$ an upper bound of the function $f_r(x)$ in $\Re$, $(1 \leq r \leq m)$.

If the system has a solution in $\Re$, then

1. There exists an $m \times 1$ integer matrix T satisfying $TD = C$; and

2. The relation

$$b_{low}(f_r, \Re) \leq c_r \leq b_{up}(f_r, \Re)$$

holds for each r in $1 \leq r \leq m$.

Algorithm 6.4.2. Let $\Re$ denote a subset of Z^n that is either a rectangle, a trapezoid, or a region that is a finite combination of trapezoids. Given a system of m linear diophantine equations

$$f_r(x) \equiv a_{r1}x_1 + a_{r2}x_2 + \cdots + a_{rn}x_n = c_r \qquad (1 \leq r \leq m)$$

in n variables, this algorithm decides if there exists a solution to the system in $\Re$. Let $A = [a_{rk}]^t$ and $C = (c_1, c_2, ..., c_m)^t$.

1. By Algorithm 5.5.1, find an $n \times n$ integer unimodular matrix U and an $n \times m$ echelon matrix D such that $UA = D$.

2. Set $r \leftarrow 1$.

3. [Generalized gcd Test.]   If an $m \times 1$ integer matrix T satisfying $TD = C$ does not exist, then the system has no solutions and the algorithm terminates. (D being an echelon matrix, the equation $TD = C$ is very easy to solve.)

4. If $\Re$ is a rectangle

$$\{(x_1, x_2, ..., x_n) \in Z^n: p_1 \leq x_1 \leq q_1, p_2 \leq x_2 \leq q_2, ..., p_n \leq x_n \leq q_n\},$$

find the minimum value $b_{low}(f_r, \mathfrak{R})$ and the maximum value $b_{up}(f_r, \mathfrak{R})$ of f_r in $\mathfrak{R}$ from the formulas

$$b_{low}(f_r, \mathfrak{R}) = \sum_{k=1}^{n} (a_{rk}^+ p_k - a_{rk}^- q_k), \quad b_{up}(f_r, \mathfrak{R}) = \sum_{k=1}^{n} (a_{rk}^+ q_k - a_{rk}^- p_k).$$

Go to step 6.

5. If $\mathfrak{R}$ is a trapezoid, find by Algorithm 4.3.1, a lower bound $b_{low}(f_r, \mathfrak{R})$ and an upper bound $b_{up}(f_r, \mathfrak{R})$ of the function f_r in the region $\mathfrak{R}$. Otherwise, $\mathfrak{R}$ can be built up from trapezoids by a finite number of operations of union and intersection. Find the bounds of f_r in $\mathfrak{R}$ by using Algorithm 4.3.1 and Lemma 4.1.2.

6. [Banerjee's Inequality.]   If c_r does not satisfy

$$b_{low}(f_r, \mathfrak{R}) \le c_r \le b_{up}(f_r, \mathfrak{R}),$$

then there is no solution to the rth equation (and hence to the system) in $\mathfrak{R}$ and the algorithm terminates.

7. Set $r \leftarrow r + 1$. If $r \le m$, go to step 2.

8. Assume the system has a solution in $\mathfrak{R}$ and terminate the algorithm.

Example 6.4.2. Consider again the problem of Example 6.4.1:

$$\begin{aligned}
&\textbf{do } I_1 = 0, 20\\
&\quad \textbf{do } I_2 = 0, 20\\
\text{S:} \quad &\qquad A(3I_1 - 2I_2 - 1, 4I_1 - 2I_2 - 4) = \cdots\\
\text{T:} \quad &\qquad \cdots = \cdots A(2I_1 + 2I_2 + 1, -3I_1 - 6I_2 + 3) \cdots\\
&\quad \textbf{enddo}\\
&\textbf{enddo}
\end{aligned}$$

This time we apply the generalized gcd test to the equations:

$$i_1 - 2i_2 - 2j_2 = 2$$
$$7i_1 - 2i_2 + 6j_2 = 7$$

The matrix **A** and the echelon matrix **D** obtained by reducing **A** are as follows:

$$A = \begin{bmatrix} 1 & 7 \\ -2 & -2 \\ -2 & -6 \end{bmatrix} \qquad D = \begin{bmatrix} 1 & 7 \\ 0 & 8 \\ 0 & 4 \end{bmatrix}.$$

There is no integer solution to the matrix equation

$$(t_1, t_2, t_3) \cdot \begin{bmatrix} 1 & 7 \\ 0 & 4 \\ 0 & 0 \end{bmatrix} = (2, 7).$$

Thus, the generalized gcd test demonstrates that there is no dependence, which Algorithm 7.4.1 could not do.

Remark 6.4.1. Algorithm 6.4.2 can be extended to provide an exact test when the rank of the echelon matrix **D** is n or (n − 1). In that case, the general (integer) solution to the matrix equation **TD** = **C**, if it exists, has at most one undetermined integer parameter. We can actually take the general solution x = **TU** to the system of equations, and then test if all constraints are satisfied. (See the Corollary to Theorem 5.5.1, and Remark 5.5.1.)

Example 6.4.3. Consider again Example 1.5 of Chapter 1:

```
        do I₁ = 1, 100
          do I₂ = 1, 50
S:           A(3*I₁ + 2, 2*I₂ − 1) = A(5*I₂, I₂ + 3) + 1
          enddo
        enddo
```

In order to decide if S depends on itself at level 1 with direction vector $(1, -1)$, we need to solve the system of linear diophantine equations

$$3i_1 - 5j_2 = -2$$
$$2i_2 - j_2 = 4,$$

where the (integer) variables satisfy the conditions

$$1 \le i_1 \le 100, \quad 1 \le i_2 \le 50$$
$$1 \le j_1 \le 100, \quad 1 \le j_2 \le 50$$
$$i_1 < j_1,$$
$$i_2 > j_2.$$

The general solution to the system of equations is

$$(i_1, i_2, j_2) = (-14 + 10t, -2 + 3t, -8 + 6t),$$

where t is any integer. Substituting for the variables in the inequalities above we get a number of inequalities in t, which are easy to solve since t is the only unknown involved. It turns out that there is no integer t satisfying all of them, so that S does not depend on itself at level 1 with direction vector $(-1, 1)$.

Remark 6.4.2. We can take the idea of Remark 6.4.1 still further as follows: Given a system of linear diophantine equations and inequalities, first partition it into smallest disjoint subsystems. (A variable appearing in an equation or inequality of one subsystem does not appear in an equation or inequality of another subsystem.) Then handle each subsystem separately. This way, we can find explicitly the general solution to the original system, in the event that each subsystem has a one-parameter solution. Even when some (at least one, but not all) subsytems have such solutions, this method could be potentially more accurate than the previous approaches. A breakup into such disjoint systems is possible if the loop bounds are constant, and the array elements are such that corresponding subscripts contain one and the same index variable, as in the loop

$$\begin{aligned}
&\textbf{do } I_1 = p_1, q_1 \\
&\quad \textbf{do } I_2 = p_2, q_2 \\
&\qquad A(a_{10} + a_{12}I_2, \; a_{20} + a_{21}I_1) = \cdots \\
&\qquad\qquad \cdots = A(b_{10} + b_{12}I_2, \; b_{20} + b_{21}I_1) \cdots \\
&\quad \textbf{enddo} \\
&\textbf{enddo}
\end{aligned}$$

We consider another example:

Example 6.4.4.

$$\begin{aligned}
&\textbf{do } I_1 = 0, 20 \\
&\quad \textbf{do } I_2 = 0, 20 \\
&\qquad \textbf{do } I_3 = 0, 20 \\
\text{S:}\quad&\qquad\quad A(I_2 - 1, \; 4*I_1 + 2, \; 3I_3 - 7) = \cdots \\
&\qquad \textbf{enddo} \\
&\qquad \textbf{do } I_4 = 0, 20 \\
\text{T:}\quad&\qquad\quad \cdots = \cdots A(3I_1 + 4, \; 2I_2 - 2, \; -2I_4 + 4) \cdots \\
&\qquad \textbf{enddo} \\
&\quad \textbf{enddo} \\
&\textbf{enddo}
\end{aligned}$$

Let us test for flow-dependence of T on S at level 2. This dependence exists iff there is an integer solution to the equations

$$\begin{aligned}
i_2 - 1 &= 3j_1 + 4 \\
4i_1 + 2 &= 2j_2 - 2 \\
3i_3 - 7 &= -2j_4 + 4
\end{aligned}$$

subject to the constraints of loop bounds (each variable must lie between 0 and 20) and the relations:

$$\begin{aligned}
i_1 &= j_1 \\
i_2 &< j_2.
\end{aligned}$$

After simplification, the equations become

$$3i_1 - i_2 = -5$$
$$4i_1 - 2j_2 = -4$$
$$3i_3 + 2j_4 = 11$$

As we saw in Example 5.5.2, they can be broken up into two disjoint subsystems: one containing the first two equations and the other containing the third. The inequalities are also broken up similarly: the ones involving i_1, i_2, j_2 go with the first subsystem; the ones in i_3, j_4 go with the second. (Note that there is no inequality that involves a variable from the set $\{i_1, i_2, j_2\}$ and a variable from the set $\{i_3, j_4\}$.) The solution to the first subsystem is

$$(i_1, i_2, j_2) = (t_1, 5 + 3t_1, 2 + 2t_1).$$

Using the (loop) bounds on these variables, we get $0 \leq t_1 \leq 5$. But, $i_2 < j_2$ yields $t_1 < -3$, so that there is no value for t_1. The solution to the second subsystem is

$$(i_3, j_4) = (11 - 2t_2, -11 + 3t_2).$$

Again, using the inequalities for these variables, we get $4 \leq t_2 \leq 5$. Thus, there is no solution to the whole system of equations and inequalities. Hence, the dependence under consideration does not exist.

6.5. MISCELLANEOUS COMMENTS

We will make a few general comments in this section. For multi-dimensional arrays, we use as a model a two-dimensional array A in a loop nest of length 2. There is no loss of generality in this; the comments can be easily translated to the general case. Consider, for example, the nest

```
do I₁= p₁, q₁
  do I₂ = p₂, q₂
    A(f(I₁, I₂),  f(I₁, I₂)) = ···
            ··· =  A(g(I₁, I₂),  g(I₁, I₂)) ···
  enddo
enddo
```

Remark 6.5.1. (Array Linearization) Given a 2-dimensional array with c-word elements $A(I_1, I_2)$ for $0 \leq I_1 \leq d_1$, $0 \leq I_2 \leq d_2$, we can store it in memory as [Knuth 1973]

$$LOC[A(I_1, I_2)] = LOC[A(0, 0)] + c*I_1 + c(d_1 + 1)*I_2.$$

Two elements $A(f_1(i_1, i_2), f_2(i_1, i_2))$ and $A(g_1(j_1, j_2), g_2(j_1, j_2))$ will be in the same memory location iff

$$LOC[A(f_1(i_1, i_2), f_2(i_1, i_2))] = LOC[A(g_1(j_1, j_2), g_2(j_1, j_2))]$$

i.e.,

$$f_1(i_1, i_2) + (d_1 + 1)*f_2(i_1, i_2) = g_1(j_1, j_2) + (d_1 + 1)*g_2(j_1, j_2). \tag{1}$$

If the subscripts are individually compared, we get the following equations:

$$f_1(i_1, i_2) = g_1(j_1, j_2)$$
$$f_2(i_1, i_2) = g_2(j_1, j_2). \tag{2}$$

The single equation (1) is equivalent to the two equations in (2). (A solution to (2) is always a solution to (1). If (1) holds, we can divide both sides by $(d_1 + 1)$ and equate remainders and quotients to derive (2). Remember that we are dealing with integer functions.) In dependence checking, an exact test that uses (1) and an exact test that uses (2) will give identical results. We have discussed the case where all subscript functions are linear, and as we have seen, even then an exact test is not always available. Linearization creates a single equation that may have more variables than there were in each of the previous equations. It may happen then that an exact test is possible before linearization, but not after. Note that the gcd test applied to (1) is really the generalized gcd test applied to the system (2), and hence is potentially better than the (regular) gcd test applied separately to each equation of (2). It is hard to predict how the result of an approximate dependence test before linearization would compare with the result of an approximate test after linearization.

In the presence of nonlinear subscript functions, it may happen that equation (1) is nonlinear, but (2) has at least one linear equation. That equation may definitely establish the lack of dependence, while given a nonlinear equation (1), the only safe thing is to assume that the dependence exists.

It is tacitly assumed above that the array bounds are not violated. If this guarantee is not there, then a solution to (1) need not be a solution to (2). If we linearize the array, do a dependence test, and find that there is no dependence, then there really is no dependence. On the other hand, if dependence is found after linearization but the subscripts could possibly violate the array bounds, then we can say nothing with certainty. Sometimes linearization is necessary, and then there may situations where it is not possible. Linearization of arrays with more than two dimensions can be discussed in a similar way. (See [Burke & Cytron 1986] and [Wolfe & Banerjee 1987]).

Remark 6.5.2. (Direction Vector Computation) When all possible direction vectors need to be computed in a particular dependence problem, we may proceed in a systematic way as explained below [Burke & Cytron 1986]:

Suppose there are only two loops containing both statements S and T. There are then nine possible direction vectors, namely,

$$(1, 1), \quad (1, 0), \quad (1, -1),$$
$$(0, 1), \quad (0, 0), \quad (0, -1),$$
$$(-1, 1), \quad (-1, 0), \quad (-1, -1).$$

First compute $(*, *)$. If this does not exist, stop. If $(*, *)$ exists, then try $(1, *)$, $(0, *)$, and $(-1, *)$. If $(1, *)$ exists, compute the three direction vector in the first row; otherwise do not compute any in that row. The other two rows are handled similarly.

Suppose direction vectors are computed for a multidimensional array by checking each subscript individually. If the collection of sets of direction vectors for individual subscripts does not have a nonempty intersection, then the corresponding dependence does not exist. For example, if we find direction vectors $\{(1, 1), (1, 0)\}$ from one subscript and $\{(0, 1), (1, -1)\}$ from another, then the correspnding dependence does not exist. (See [Wolfe 1982], [Wolfe and Banerjee 1987]).

Remark 6.5.3. (Extension of the Program Model)
Loop Normalization: If we have a loop of the form

$$\textbf{do } I = p, q, r$$
$$\vdots$$
$$\textbf{enddo}$$

where the increment r is not 1, we introduce a new index variable J $= (I - p)/r$, replace each occurrence of I in the body with $(p + rJ)$, and thereby transform the given loop into the *normalized* loop

$$\textbf{do } J = 0, (q - p)/r, 1$$
$$\vdots$$
$$\textbf{enddo}$$

which fits our model. Normalization may be applied explicitly to the loop or implicitly during the dependence testing phase. In a situation like

$$\textbf{do } I_1 = p_1, q_1$$
$$\textbf{do } I_2 = p_2, q_2, r_2$$
$$\vdots$$
$$\textbf{enddo}$$
$$\textbf{enddo}$$

if p_2 contains I_1, normalization of the inner loop may make the array-subscripts in the body more complex. To reduce the need for normalization, we did not use a simple lower limit of 0 or 1 in our model program.

Remark 6.5.4. (Generalized Dependence Problem) Finally, we would like to end with some general observations on the dependence problem and the various approaches to its solution. Consider a set of m equations

$$f_r(\mathbf{x}) = 0 \qquad\qquad (r = 1, 2,..., m)$$

in n variables $x_1, x_2,..., x_n$, where $h_1, h_2,..., h_m$ are real valued functions on $\mathbf{R}^n$. Let S_{int} denote the set of integer solutions and S_{rel} the set of real solutions to the system. Also, let $S_{i,int}$ denote the set of integer solutions and $S_{i,rel}$ the set of real solutions to the rth equation alone, $(r = 1, 2,..., m)$. It is then clear that

$$\begin{aligned} S_{int} &= \mathbf{Z}^n \cap S_{rel}, \\ S_{int} &= \cap \{S_{i,int} : 1 \leq r \leq m\}, \\ S_{rel} &= \cap \{S_{i,rel} : 1 \leq r \leq m\}. \end{aligned}$$

and

Take any nonempty subset $\mathfrak{R}$ of $\mathbf{R}^n$. We use $S_{int}(\mathfrak{R})$ to denote the set of all integer solutions to the system in $\mathfrak{R}$, and the symbols $S_{rel}(\mathfrak{R})$, $S_{r,int}(\mathfrak{R})$, $S_{r,rel}(\mathfrak{R})$ are to be interpreted in a similar way. It follows trivially that

$$S_{int}(\mathfrak{R}) = S_{int} \cap \mathfrak{R}, \qquad S_{rel}(\mathfrak{R}) = S_{rel} \cap \mathfrak{R},$$

$$S_{r,int}(\mathfrak{R}) = S_{r,int} \cap \mathfrak{R}, \qquad S_{r,rel}(\mathfrak{R}) = S_{r,rel} \cap \mathfrak{R}.$$

The problem of deciding whether the system of equations has an integer solution in $\mathfrak{R}$, i.e., whether the set $S_{int}(\mathfrak{R})$ is nonempty, can be approached in several ways. We consider a number of them in the following. The first two are exact methods. Methods III through VI are approximate methods in the sense that they test only necessary conditions for the nonemptiness of $S_{int}(\mathfrak{R})$. Each of them tests a superset of $S_{int}(\Re)$ for possible emptiness. If the superset is empty, $S_{int}(\Re)$ must be empty. When the superset is nonempty, $S_{int}(\Re)$ may or may not be empty; we assume in this case that it is empty.

METHOD I. Decide directly if $S_{int}(\Re)$ is empty.

METHOD II. Find the set S_{int} and decide if $S_{int} \cap \Re$ is empty, i.e., find all integer solutions to the system, and then test which ones lie in $\Re$, if any.

METHOD III. $S_{int}(\Re) \subset S_{int}$. Determine if the system has an integer solution (anywhere in $\mathbf{Z}^n$).

METHOD IV. $S_{int}(\Re) \subset S_{r,int}$ for each r. Determine if each individual equation has an integer solution.

METHOD V. $S_{int}(\Re) \subset S_{rel}(\Re)$. Determine if the system has a real solution in $\Re$.

METHOD VI. $S_{int}(\Re) \subset S_{r,rel}(\Re)$ for each r. Determine if each individual equation has a real solution in $\Re$.

Note that Method III is stronger (potentially more accurate) than IV, since $S_{int}(\Re) \subset S_{int} \subset S_{r,int}$ for each r; and for similar reasons V is stronger than VI. We have omitted two more supersets of $S_{int}(\Re)$, namely S_{rel} and $S_{r,rel}$.

Assume now that each function h_r is linear, i.e., of the form

$$h_r(\mathbf{x}) = a_{r1}x_1 + a_{r2}x_2 + \cdots + a_{rn}x_n - c_r$$

where the a_{rk}'s and c_r's are integer constants, and the region $\Re$ is defined by a set of linear inequalities in $x_1, x_2,..., x_n$. We can make a number of points:

1. We saw in Chapter 5 that the general solution to a system of linear diophantine equations can be expressed as linear combina-

tions of a number of arbitrary integral parameters. Using these expressions to fit the constraints of $\Re$ yields a set of inequalities in those parameters. This system of inequalities can be solved if it turns out that no more than one parameter is present in each. Algorithm 6.2.1 and the algorithms indicated in Remark 6.4.1 fall in this category. The advantage of this method over the others is that here we can find closed-form expressions for the general solution in $\Re$, if any solution exists.

2. The gcd tests of Section 6.3 illustrate Method III, and Algorithm 6.4.1 is Method IV. The generalized gcd test of Algorithm 6.4.2 is also Method III.

3. The inequality tests of Section 6.3 constitute Method V when the bounds are actually extreme values. The inequality tests of algorithms 6.4.1 and 6.4.2 represent Method VI.

4. An example of Method I is integer programming.

5. Other examples of Method V include linear programming methods and Shostack's method of loop residues [Shostak 1981].

A complete discussion of all these methods and their relative merits is beyond the scope of the present book.

REFERENCES

Allen, J. R. 1983. Dependence Analysis for Subscripted Variables and Its Application to Program Transformations. Ph.D. Dissertation, Department of Mathematical Sciences, Rice University, Houston, Texas (April). Also available as document 83-14916 from University Microfilms, Ann Arbor, Michigan.

Allen, J. R., and Kennedy, K. 1984. Automatic Loop Interchange. In *Conference Proceedings —The SIGPLAN '84 Symposium on Compiler Construction* (Montreal, Canada, June 17–22). Also available as *SIGPLAN Notices*, Vol. 19, No. 6 (June), pp. 233–246.

Allen, J. R., and Kennedy, K. 1987. Automatic Translation of FORTRAN Programs to Vector Form. *ACM Transactions on Programming Languages & Systems*, Vol. 9, No. 4 (October), pp. 491–542. (The earliest version of this appeared in October, 1980 as a Rice University Technical Report.)

Allen, J. R., Kennedy, K., Porterfield, C., and Warren, J. 1983. Conversion of Control Dependence to Data Dependence. In *Conference Proceedings —The 10th AnnualACM Symposium on Principles of Programming Languages* (Austin, Texas, January 24–26), ACM Press, pp.177–189.

Banerjee, U. 1976. Data Dependence in Ordinary Programs. M.S. Thesis, Report 76-837, Department of Computer Science, University of Illinois at Urbana-Champaign, Urbana, Illinois (November).

149

Banerjee, U. 1979. Speedup of Ordinary Programs. Ph.D. Dissertation, Report 79-989, Department of Computer Science, University of Illinois at Urbana-Champaign, Urbana, Illinois (October). Also available as document 80-08967 from University Microfilms, Ann Arbor, Michigan.

Banerjee, U. 1988. An Introduction to a Formal Theory of Dependence Analysis. *The Journal of Supercomputing* (to appear).

Banerjee, U., Chen, S. C., Kuck, D. J., and Towle, R. A. 1979. Time and Parallel Processor Bounds for Fortran-like Loops. *IEEE Transactions on Computers*, Vol. C-28, No. 9 (September), pp. 660–670.

Burke, M., and Cytron, R. 1986. Interprocedural Dependence Analysis and Parallelization. In *Conference Proceedings — The SIGPLAN '86 Symposium on Compiler Construction* (Palo Alto, California, June 25–27). Also available as *SIGPLAN Notices*, Vol. 21, No. 7 (July), pp. 162–175.

Cohagan, W. L. 1973. Vector Optimization for the ASC. In *Conference Proceedings —The 7th Annual Princeton Conference on Information Sciences and Systems* (Princeton, New Jersey, March 22–23), Princeton University Press, pp. 169–174.

Fan, K. 1956. On Systems of Linear Inequalities. *Annals of Mathematics Studies*, No. 38. Princeton University Press, Princeton, New Jersey, pp. 99–156.

Halmos, P. R. 1965. *Naive Set Theory*. D. Van Nostrand, Princeton, New Jersey.

Kertzner, S. 1981. The Linear Diophantine Equation. *American Mathematical Monthly*, Vol. 88, No. 3 (March), pp. 200–203.

Kirch, A. M. 1974. *Elementary Number Theory*, Intext, New York, NY.

Knuth, D. E. 1973. *The Art of Computer Programming*, Vol. 1, *Fundamental Algorithms*, Second Edition, Addison-Wesley, Reading, Massachusetts.

Knuth, D. E. 1981. *The Art of Computer Programming*, Vol. 2, *Seminumerical Algorithms*, Second Edition, Addison-Wesley, Reading, Massachusetts.

Kuck, D. J., Kuhn, R. H., Padua, D. A., Leasure, B. R., and Wolfe, M. J. 1981. Dependence Graphs and Compiler Optimizations. In *Conference Proceedings —The 8th ACM Symposium on Principles of Programming Languages* (Williamsburgh, Virginia, January 26–28), ACM Press, pp. 207–218.

Kuhn, R. H. 1980. Optimization and Interconnection Complexity for : Parallel Processors, Single-Stage Networks, and Decision Trees. Ph.D. Dissertation, Report 80-1009, Department of Computer Science, University of Illinois at Urbana-Champaign, Urbana, Illinois (February). Also available as document 80-26541 from University Microfilms, Ann Arbor, Michigan.

Lamport, L. 1974. The Parallel Execution of DO Loops. *Communications of ACM*, Vol. 17, No. 2 (February), pp. 83–93.

Mordell, L. J. 1969. *Diophantine Equations*. Academic Press, New York, New York.

Padua, D. A., and Wolfe, M. J. 1986. Advanced Compiler Optimizations for Supercomputers. *Communications of the ACM*, Vol. 29, No. 12 (December), pp. 1184–1201.

Shostak, R. 1981. Deciding Linear Inequalities by Computing Loop Residues. *Journal of the ACM*, Vol. 28, No. 4 (October), pp. 769–779.

Towle, R. A. 1976. Control and Data Dependence for Program Transformations. Ph.D. Dissertation, Report 76-788, Department of Computer Science, University of Illinois at Urbana-Champaign, Urbana, Illinois (March).

Wolfe, M. J. 1982. Optimizing Supercompilers for Supercomputers. Ph.D. Dissertation, Report 82-1105, Department of Computer Science, University of Illinois at Urbana-Champaign, Urbana, Illinois (October). Also available as document 83-03027 from University Microfilms, Ann Arbor, Michigan.

Wolfe, M. J., and Banerjee, U. 1987. Data Dependence and Its Application to Parallel Processing. *International Journal of Parallel Programming*, Vol. 16, No. 2 (April), pp. 137–178.

INDEX

assignment statement 20

Banerjee's inequality 113, 116
b_{low} 57, 64
b_{up} 57, 64

dependence 28
    anti-dependence 28, 29
    approximate test 102
    associated iteration pair 29
    at depth 30
    at level 29
    (with) direction vector 30
    (with) distance vector 30
    exact test 101
    flow-dependence 28, 29
    graph 34
    indirect 34
    level graph 34
    output-dependence 28, 29
    problem 36
        generalized 146
diophantine equation 57
    connected 90
    directly connected 90
    disjoint 90
    system 85
direction vector 18
distance vector 18